# FROM OAKS TO AVOCETS

# FROM OAKS TO AVOCETS

John Walling

**Memoirs**

Published by Riparian Publishing
5 Tonnant Way
Grimsby

ISBN 0 9523848 0 9

Typesetting by Riverhead Typesetters Ltd    Grimsby
Printed in Great Britain by  Antony Rowe Ltd. ,   Chippenham. Wiltshire.

To
My Grandchildren
Martin
Kerry and Tracy

# ACKNOWLEDGEMENTS.

I would like to thank Kate and Eileen for their patience and support in the early stages, and a special thank-you to Ernest Corbett for his expert advice.

# LIST OF ILLUSTRATIONS

# SOURCES CONSULTED

Odhams History of the Second World War.      Chapters 1 and 4

Atherstone: An Outline History of a North
Warwickshire Market Town. ed. J. L. Salter,
(Atherstone Local History Research Group)      Chapter 3

History of the Second World War - 'The War
Against Japan. Vol 1' - Her Majesty's
Stationery Office 1957.      Chapter 5

History of the Life and Reign of Richard
the Third - James Gairdner.      Chapter 10

History of Burton Upon Trent. Part 1.
  Dennis Stuart.      Chapter 11

A Short History of Boston. ed H. W. Nicholson.      Chapter 11

Photograph of Toll Gate House .... with kind permission of M. J. Alexander
(Atherstone Local History Research Group)

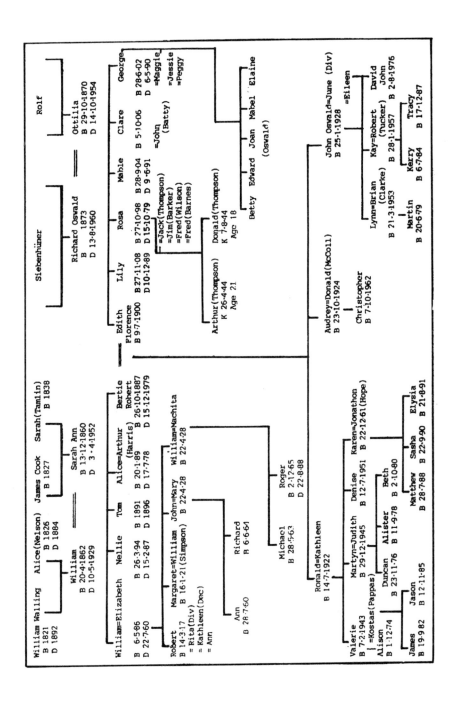

# CONTENTS

# INTRODUCTION

I often thought how I would have enjoyed reading an account by my grandpa, of what life was like when he was a boy; what he did when a young man and how his life and times changed throughout his 85 years. This prompted me to write my life story and if my grandchildren have similar desires, then they will have the answers in this book.

I was fortunate to have had a happy childhood and looking back, I think of the summers always being sunny and warm, the winters cold with long periods of snow. Sometimes the canal would freeze over and the coal-laden boats, laboriously pulled by a lean horse straining in its harness, would cut through the ice until it became too thick for them to move. In the same year the reservoir at Oldbury would also be covered in ice, thick enough to skate on. When it rained, the thunderstorms brought torrents of rain gushing down Coleshill Road past our house, to flood the road lower down and the cellar of "The Maid of the Mill" public house. Someone would then lift the clogged-up drain grill cover so that the rain water could escape and the flood subside.

Did this happen every year or was it only two or three times?

The kitchen on Monday morning was full of activity: washing boiling in the "set-pot" in the corner, the room full of steam, and soapy bubbling water lifting up the wooden lid, slurping out and spitting against the hot cast-iron door of the coal fire beneath, and splashing on to the red-tiled floor. Outside in the yard there was the rhythmic drumming as the long-handled wooden dolly pounded the washing in the galvanised tub. Water spilled everywhere and ran from the rollers of the huge cast iron mangle, as the thickly-folded sheets were fed through after first being rinsed in cold water. Then when they were pegged out on the rope line down the garden path, blowing and drying in the wind, mother would get annoyed after all her hard work as they caught on the overhanging branches of the apple trees next door, leaving dirty marks on the white bed-linen. On rainy days, the clothes-horse would be round the fire in the kitchen or living room, and there was a pleasant fresh damp smell of washing drying.

The Outwoods, on the edge of the old Forest of Arden, was a large area of common land where I spent many happy hours playing, often alone. A number of ancient oak trees stood majestically on the grassy slopes from 'the level' down towards the cowpastures, and one – where the red clay soil had eroded from the thick gnarled roots – was known as the 'Devil's Cave'. During the summer months, I would sit sometimes on the hill under the trees opposite the home of Mr. Stafford, the hat manufacturer, watching people play tennis on the courts by the side of the house. During severe weather when I was unable to go out, I would get out a drawing book or do the circular " Daily Mail" jig-saw of "Dogs" as the rain poured down, visible against the black-painted gable-end of the house diagonally opposite the bay window of our 'front-room'.

My bedroom, which I shared with my elder brother, looked out over the gardens and distant houses towards Merevale Park. In the calm summer evenings the eerie "meowing" call of the peacocks at Merevale Hall mingled with the "caw" and "caah" of the rooks, nesting in the tall trees on the other side of the high stone wall which bordered the park. This wall, and a brick one that joined it along Watling Street, ran the whole length of the Atherstone side of the park, from the bottom of Merevale Lane to opposite the old Toll-Gate house at the back of the Outwoods in Coleshill Road.

I walked many miles with my mother along the country lanes

around Atherstone, looking for a wall she claimed to have seen some years earlier. We never found it and I became convinced that it had only existed in one of her many related dreams! We also went blackberrying together and with the "fallens" from Mr. Wood's apple trees next door, she would make blackberry and apple jam. She often also made her own bread and sometimes I would help by mixing with a spoon the yeast and the sugar until it magically turned to liquid.

Then the dough was put into a large earthenware pot covered with a cloth and placed in the hearth where the warmth of the fire would cause it to rise.

At the week-end I would run up the road to Horton's corner shop and press my nose to the window selecting the sweets that I could buy with my Saturday penny – a small paper bag of fruit sherbets perhaps and a chocolate covered toffee "Peg-Bar". They would last me all day. During the week Dad would miraculously produce a sweet from his pocket for me. I never realised at the time that it was often the same one that I had given to him the Saturday before! As a treat, I would perhaps be allowed a small piece of delicious candied peel or an extra spoonful of our daily ration of the sticky cod-liver-oil-and-malt.

We bought our groceries from the Co-op, (Co-operative Wholesale Society) only a few yards down the road, and took them home neatly wrapped in a brown paper parcel. On the counter was a large reel of thick black twist tobacco for pipe smokers. It was also bought by coal miners for chewing when they were underground to keep the dust out of their throats. At the end of their night shift or in the afternoon, the miners could be seen returning home from Baddesley Colliery, with their hands and faces still black from working in those dreadful conditions. They had no pit baths in those early days.

Sometimes before they cleaned themselves up, they'd have to shovel and wheelbarrow their coal supply into their coal-houses from where it had been tipped up in the road. This free coal allowance for miners began as a type of bonus given by the mine owners, and the amount varied depending on how much coal was "turned" in a shift. After nationalization, it was continued as part of the wages structure, with miners getting 10cwt a month, deputies 15cwt, and overmen 1 ton.

Opposite the Co-op, Bindley's Off Licence sold beer straight from the barrel, which was collected in jugs usually by women, and there was a house in Stanley Road which sold home-made faggots in gravy to those people requiring an inexpensive meal.

Sunday School Treats were held in the grounds of Atherstone Hall, and the Co-op Treat in the field opposite the Senior School in Witherley Road, where the Wholesale Society grazed their horses. During the sports activities held on that day, we gave our Co-op number – 748 in my case – in exchange for a bag of sandwiches, an iced bun and a small bottle of lemonade.

The milk-float and bread-van were both pulled by horses and so was Mrs. Thorpe's ice-cream cart. Mr. Pitman brought the milk to the door in a galvanized can and used his half-pint, pint or quart ladle to put the milk straight into mother's large pot jug. Then he would refill the container from one of the 12 gallon churns he had on the float. Ted brought the bread also to the door in a wicker-basket over his arm and Mrs. Thorpe's ice-cream was the "nicest in the world".

Dad was on the staff at Wilson and Stafford's Hat Factory as a warehouseman, bringing home four pounds-ten shillings a week – a good wage in the 1930s.

Life was good. We were a happy family.

# CHAPTER ONE

# IN THE WARS

I was born on 25 January 1928 in the small market town of Atherstone in North Warwickshire, the youngest of three children. My sister Audrey was born on October 23 1924 and my brother Ronald on July 14 1922 – both in Leeds.

My childhood was eventful, mainly through an impetuous nature and taking uncalculated risks. As a result I broke my arm twice, was knocked down by a car (not really hurt), fell into the Coventry Canal after slipping from broken ice, and fell down a tree landing on my knee. This last episode necessitated a month's stay in Nuneaton Hospital to repair torn ligaments. All this before my 12th birthday! However, in spite of these painful experiences, memories of my childhood are of a very happy period of my life, due no doubt, to the love and security given to all three of us by our parents.

My education, such as it was, began at the North Street Infants School. Although we began by learning the three 'Rs', the only thing I can clearly recall was the obligatory 'arms on desks and heads down' nap during the afternoon. I then attended the mixed South Junior School in Owen Street, where we played at the opposite end of the playground from the girls. As we marched in single file into the school, the headmaster, "Daddy" Essam, would stand unsmiling by the closed gate, hands behind his back, on the lookout for late-comers. The sweet pleasant aroma of the smoke from his pipe spread across the playground and into the classrooms.

We handed in our 'milk money' on Monday mornings, $2^1/_2$ pence per week (equivalent to about 1p today) for our daily one-third-of-a-pint of creamy milk. Pushing the straw through a small hole in the cardboard top, there would be a race to see who was the first to finish. Miss West read to us children's stories and classics in abundance. We learned about poor little Tom and the Water Babies, the one legged Steadfast Tin Soldier who was in love with his ballerina, and the Darling children who flew out of their bedroom window with Peter Pan and Tinkerbell. We heard about Gulliver and the Lilliputians, the Just So Stories of Rudyard Kipling and many others. I believe many children today know little about these lovely imaginative stories which taught us so much more than just how to read.

When we sat for the 11 plus exam, it was said that an IQ of over 120 was required for entry to the only Grammar School in the town. This was no doubt due to the very large catchment area, and that the available places were reduced by fee-paying pupils. From over 90 children of my year, from the North and South Junior Schools, only one passed for the Grammar School, although many sat the examination. The later chance at age 13 was thwarted because of overcrowding, due to girls from Stoke Park and Barrs Hill Schools from Coventry, being evacuated to Atherstone because of the war and accommodated at the school.

The standard of education at the Senior School where I spent the next 3 years was poor, but possibly in those first years of the war, the catastrophic events which were happening in Europe influenced what we were taught. We had no language lessons apart from English, and our Maths teacher preferred to give us books to read on farming. We learned how to breed flocks of Cheviot Sheep and raise Highland cattle, but apart from some elementary mathematics, little else I recall. On fine days, he would select a few of us to do a little gardening on the school plot. This possibly was in response to the Government's direction of 'Digging for Victory', when people were encouraged to grow their own vegetables wherever possible. So in addition to maths – including a brief introduction to algebra – and farming, I also learned how to dig!

We enjoyed our 'Singing Lessons' and so did our teacher. To our amusement he would occasionally lapse into reciting light verse such as, "There was a man who had two sons. . " (to a piano accompaniment), or perhaps sing a Victorian Ballad, "The Soldier's Farewell". I believe he performed these in his local pub at weekends. However, we did learn and sing "Who is Sylvia?", "The Holy City", Annie Laurie", and an English translation of Schubert's "Haiden-Roslein" and a complete new version of Verdi's "La Donna e Mobile" from his opera "Rigoletto", which we knew as "Moonlight and Melody".

The school leaving age was then fourteen, and I left at Easter 1942, a couple of months after my birthday, and started work immediately as a junior clerk at Mancetter Granite Quarries. Fortunately, I was able to continue with my education attending Nuneaton Technical College with a view to sitting for my National Certificate later on. I attended the college on a one day a week basis thanks to my employers but when I was 17 years old, I volunteered for the Royal Naval Air Service (RNAS), eventually joining HMS 'Royal Arthur' at Skegness (Butlins Holiday Camp before the war), on August 14th 1945.

The next day, Japan surrendered unconditionally and the war was over!

However, World War 2 was still some two years ahead when I celebrated my 9th birthday. We had a very wet Spring that year, and the rain continued well into May. An enormous bonfire built in the Outwoods got a good soaking from the constant rain. In the hollow space beneath, paper and cardboard were packed into it at the last moment before the fire was lit on 12th May. Many others throughout the country were lit at the same time to mark the Coronation of our new King, George VI, and Queen Elizabeth. A book entitled 'George VI – King and Emperor' with a royal blue cover, was presented to all pupils in the town of Atherstone and included a Foreword from the Chairman of the Parish Council, John Stringer, the Vice Chairman, Arthur Hargrave and the Parish Clerk, E. S. Sands. Captain Sands, a distinguished soldier of the 1914-18 War, was later to become a Commanding Officer of the local Home Guard during the Second World War.

The foreword carried a message to all children, telling us, ". . . . . . . . the Coronation is the greatest moment in every monarch's reign, when as the coronation ring symbolises, the Sovereign and the country are wedded to each other and it was hoped that this book, written about the First Citizen and Head of our Empire, would help the schoolboys and schoolgirls of Great and Greater Britain, who are growing up to take their places in the Commonwealth of Nations. . . . to a better understanding of what citizenship means".

We were only two years older when war was declared against Germany and the nations of the world were divided, but the British Empire as we knew it then, with the same man as King and Emperor of that Empire, was united in its resolve to defeat the enemy by war.

During the year previous to 1937, we had been ruled by an un-crowned king. Even as an 8 year old, I was aware of the dramatic events of that year and that an American woman was somehow preventing our king from taking the throne. At Christmas time our carols included a satirical version of one of the most widely sung of them. "Hark the Herald Angels Sing. . . . Mrs Simpson stole our King!" It was, of course, impossible for the king to marry a divorcee.

4

Edward VIII had made known his decision to abdicate in a wireless broadcast which we listened to as a family. Dad making rude remarks throughout the speech making us laugh, referring to Mrs Simpson as "that woman". Mum, however, looked very serious and in common with many other women at the time, I believe, silently admired a king's courage in taking such a momentous step for the love of a woman. I was too young to fully understand the significance of what he said but I can still recall him clearly stating that he had, ". . . found it impossible to carry the heavy burden of responsibility and to discharge my duties as King as I would wish to do, without the help and support of the woman I love".

Having been denied a Coronation in that year, now we were to have a real one and I thought that the most important part of the proceedings was to guard the bonfire in the Outwoods at Atherstone. Had I been confronted by hooligans intent on vandalising the structure, there must have been very little that a 9 year old Wolf-Cub could have done to prevent it. Nevertheless, it remained intact due, we believed, to the vigilance of the 1st and 2nd Atherstone Scouts and Cubs. Considering the wet weather, it would have been extremely difficult if not impossible to set it alight anyway. Even on the day when it was eventually lit in great ceremony by the Group Scoutmaster, Ted Comley, it took a long time to get hold, even after being secretly and liberally soaked with paraffin – not very "scouty" but necessary. When it started to burn, the flames lit up the night sky and showers of sparks carried by the wind, caused the crowds to move further back. We began to fear for our bell-tents although they were some distance away, indeed it was so great that the huge logs at the base of the fire were still burning next morning round the outside of a large pile of grey ash. The area was surrounded by a mound of turf where the ground had been levelled and was marked for years afterwards. Water settled on the surface to create a small pond and later, as drainage took place, the new grass was a lusher green than the surrounding area.

Some four years later, from roughly the same spot, my brother and I were to watch the red glow in the sky some 12 miles away, as Coventry burned in the blitz.

I was 11 years old when war was declared on September 3rd 1939. It was a Sunday. We all sat in the front room, listening to the announcement on the wireless by the Prime Minister, Neville Chamberlain, as he broadcast to the nation from 10 Downing Street:

"This morning the British Ambassador in Berlin handed the German Government a final note, stating that unless we heard from them by 11 o'clock that they were prepared at once to withdraw their troops from Poland, a state of war would exist between us. I have to tell you now that no such undertaking has been received and consequently, this country is at war with Germany".

Dad looked serious, Mother sighed and Ron and I sniggered. The solemnity of the occasion caused us to do so. It had, of course, been only 21 years since the ending of the First World War with all its horrific memories for our parents, but all this meant nothing to us and we certainly didn't feel threatened. In fact, I believed that it was the beginning of a great new adventure.

And to me, a young boy still at school, it was. When we learned about the "Miracle of Dunkirk" and listened to one of J. B. Priestley's 'Post-scripts' on the wireless, telling about the little boats and ships going across the English Channel to rescue our army from the beaches of that French port, it was like a story straight out of the weekly paper-back magazines that were popular at that time – the Wizard or the Hotspur. I cut out the maps from the 'Daily Mail' following with interest the advancing armies in the North Africa campaigns, the invasion of Sicily and Italy by the Allied Armies and eventually France.

In September 1939, the commencement of the school term was delayed for a week. Soon afterwards, regular rehearsals took place of going into the partly underground Air-Raid shelters in the grounds of the school. The only light which penetrated the darkness of those cold brick shelters, apart from the central doorway, was at each end when we partly lifted the emergency exit covers. This was a favourite place to be, especially for those not fond of the dark. I used to get there, however, for a different reason. The little bit of light enabled me to read the words of some risque songs I had written down from gramophone records. My renderings of "With me gloves in me 'and and me 'at on one side. . ", or George Formby's "Oh don't the Wind Blow Cold", I sang to the amusement of the others but no doubt to the surprise of the teachers. However, I was allowed to continue my 'performances' until visits to the shelters ceased when it was considered unnecessary to continue with the exercise.

When food rationing was introduced early in 1940, it had little or no effect on the family's eating habits. One and a quarter pounds of both butter and bacon, and three and three quarter pounds of sugar was sufficient for our family of five, providing we were careful[1]. Even when meat was rationed a couple of months later to just under ten shillings' worth (50p) per week, it caused little hardship. After all, ten shillings represented about an eighth of mother's weekly house-keeping. Our milkman, Mr Pitman, had told us when war was declared that it would be all over by Christmas but when France fell in the following June and England stood alone against Hitler's domination of Europe, we knew that the war would be a long affair.

On the 10th May 1940, the day when Holland and Belgium were invaded, the Prime Minister, Neville Chamberlain resigned, and Winston Churchill formed an all-party National Government. After the failure of Chamberlain as a war leader, Churchill inspired and rallied the Nation with his stirring and defiant speeches. The day after the fall of France he told us that we were,

". . . . the sole champion now in arms to defend the world cause. We shall do our best to be worthy of that honour. We shall defend

---

[1]   Later on in 1940 food rationing was further reduced to 2oz butter, 8oz sugar, 2oz tea, 1oz cheese, 4oz margarine and 2oz cooking fat per person.

our island and with the British Empire around us, we shall fight on unconquerable, until the curse of Hitler is lifted from the brows of men".

In the middle of July the German Luftwaffe began their air offensive in the Battle of Britain which continued until October, but at first we saw little or nothing of it in the Midlands; the air battles and bombing were mainly concentrated in the south of the country. However, when the bombing started in the Midlands towards the end of 1940, things were a little different. Although bombs fell on neighbouring Nuneaton and nearby cities, none actually fell on buildings in Atherstone. At night the sirens would sound and we would sit under the stairs, reputed to be the safest place if the house collapsed, and hear the distant sounds of explosions over in Coventry and the outskirts of Birmingham. It became routine but I didn't enjoy my sleep being disturbed just to sit there in the cold, apparently in no real danger.

Gradually I became more reluctant to join the others, until eventually, the calls to 'come down' fell on deaf ears. One night I was aware of an increasingly loud 'whistle' of bombs falling. I sat bolt upright in bed, following the descending sound with eyes wide open, seeing nothing. Blind terror drove me to establish the record for the fastest time from the back bedroom to the hall during the war, arriving there before the bombs hit the ground about two miles away!

Occasionally news came that someone we knew had been killed or reported 'missing'. Frank Jarvis, who had lived with his parents only four doors away, was killed early in the war in France. Alf Moores, who had lived opposite our house, was one of the many servicemen captured and held prisoner until the war ended. My Aunt Rosa's two boys from Leeds, sadly lost their lives within six months of each other. Arthur was blown up in a tank in Imphal, Burma, and Donald drowned off the invasion beaches soon after D-Day whilst serving in the Navy. I was too young to know all of the local men killed between the years 1939-1945 but I knew some. In the bar of the 'Black Horse' in Long Street, one wall was covered for years with photographs of some of the men of Atherstone who had died in the war – familiar faces, faces that never changed their youthful looks. I still remember my cousins Arthur and Donald as I hear the words spoken from Binyon's Requiem every Armistice Sunday: – "They shall grow not old, as we that are left grow old, Age shall not weary them nor the years condemn, At the going down of the sun and in the morning We will remember them".

I enjoyed being in uniform, as many young men did in those days. It probably started when I was 8 years old, the earliest age I was able to join the cubs. This was followed by three more years in the Scouts, then three years in the ATC (Air Training Corps) and finally, two years in Naval uniform.

I had had a yearning to be in the Cubs from the day I saw the local Scout Band marching along Coleshill Road. I would only have been about 6 years old as I walked along by the side of them, not looking where I was going and colliding with a lamp-post! I loved Scouting, and after leaving the Navy, I was connected with the Scout Movement in one way or another, for the next 35 years. Despite my love of Scouting however, I left them to join the 1162 (Anker)Squadron of the ATC because I wanted to go into the RAF or Fleet Air Arm when I became old enough. The Air Training Corps was formed in February 1941 with the sole purpose of acting as a reservoir from which these two Services could draw its future air and ground crews. The RAF was my first choice. However, I had been unsuccessful in an interview at Bristol for RAF aircrew, so instead sat an Selection Test at Coventry with another ATC cadet from Atherstone. The result of the Test, which was announced to us before we left, gave me the choice of either to be a 'Writer' (administrative job) or 'Air Mechanic – Engines' in the Fleet Air Arm (or as it had been renamed, The Royal Naval Air Service). I decided to have a change from office work and chose 'Air

Mechanic'.

The three and a half years I spent in the ATC introduced me to a whole range of new and interesting subjects: as well as learning Aircraft Recognition, Morse, Navigation, some Astronomy and Meteorology, it also gave me a wider knowledge in Maths. In addition I had flights in an Avro 'Anson', Airspeed 'Oxford' and the Vickers-Armstrong 'Wellington' all with aircrew on training missions. We flew from the aerodrome at Lindley, near Fenny Drayton, about four miles east of Atherstone. Some of us were invited by an American crew to 'take a trip' with them to Turnhill in Shropshire, quite unofficially, in their 'Dakota'.

"You'll be back in a couple of hours or so – don't need parachutes – like ridin' in a 'bus," they told us.

We accepted their offer but were reprimanded by our officers when we arrived back for going without permission or parachutes.

Being in uniform and mixing with the Service personnel in the NAAFI gave us the feeling that we were already in the RAF and everyone appeared to be having a wonderful time.

We were a long way away from the horrors of the war!

# CHAPTER TWO

# DEAR NELSON

My father was born in Liverpool in 1887, the second eldest of five children. His brother, Uncle Will, was a year older than my father, but his other brother, Tom Winstanley, born in May 1891, lived only 4 years and 7 months. There were also two sisters, Helen (Nellie) and Alice. The family had moved to the Leeds area when Dad was quite small. Uncle Will and Dad married but Alice had only six years of married life. When her husband died in 1937, Auntie Nellie and Grandma went to live with her. Grandma died in 1952 aged 92. She was a grand old lady with lovely white hair and always proud of her appearance. Widowed when she was 69, she became very deaf in later years. Her pre-war ear trumpet was replaced by a sort of 'speaking tube'. This was a flexible pipe with a mouth piece at one end and an ear plug at the other. With a wave of a hand she would be asked to 'plug in' when anyone wanted to speak to her, but if you raised your voice she would remove the plug from her ear and retort, "Don't shout, I'm not deaf!" When she was in her 80's she broke her thigh after a fall and never fully recovered, being bed-ridden until her death.

If it was a fine day she would look thoughtful and remark, "I wish I was in Brid'" and then give a little smile as she remembered an outing or holiday she had had at Bridlington. The house they lived in belonged to Auntie Alice who chatted constantly to her pet budgie and canary. 'Mickey' the budgie was a good talker and on one occasion soon after my father had arrived in the house during a visit, he interrupted the conversation with, "Our Bertie's come, our Bertie's come, sweetheart Bertie". Auntie's perseverance in teaching him the phrase had paid off at the right moment. Unable to get the right type of seed during the war however, Mickey died and it was said that the canary hardly ever sang again. In 1964, when I left Atherstone, Alice sold her house and the two Aunties came to live in the house I had vacated, in order to be nearer their brother.

Dad had been a delicate child, born with a less severe form of spina-bifida, a malformation of the vertebrae in his lumbar region which caused him some discomfort throughout his life and he was 5 years old before he started walking. In 1934 a serious internal haemorrhage increased the size of the lump which he had always had on his back, to huge proportions. It re-occurred even more severely in 1937 and he underwent a long and painful operation in Nuneaton General Hospital, performed by a Mr. Rasen assisted by our family GP Mr. Pracy, also a surgeon, to repair the damaged spine. Soon afterwards, in an attempt to 'tidy up' the wound where the operation had taken place, a skin graft taken from his thigh proved to be unsuccessful. Although the repair to the spine apparently prevented any further problems, an accident when he was 70 caused the wound to re-open. A motor-cyclist had lost control of his machine, mounted the pavement and hit my father causing bruising and breaking his ankle. When the bone healed, it was decided to do a skin graft on his back over the place where the previous operation in 1937 had been. The new technique, pioneered by Dr. Archie McIndoe in dealing with badly burned RAF aircrew during the war, was used. It took seven operations to move a large flap of skin from his abdomen in such a way that it always remained attached to his body in order for the blood vessels to keep it alive, until it was eventually brought round to a position where it could be placed over the affected area. This time it was successful but was quite an ordeal for him to endure at over 70 years of age.

At 12 years old he was the smallest boy in the choir at St. Columba's Church and had a sweet treble voice. At that time the family lived in an old house in the village of Busley, about 4 miles from Leeds City centre. Auntie Nellie recalled to me, a typical Christmas she had had in about the year 1900, when she was 7 and Dad 13. The Minister at the Atherstone Congregational Church had asked her to tell the Sunday School children (she was aged 90 at the time) what life was like when she was a little girl and she repeated to me the story she told them.

"I went to bed very early on Christmas Eve and hung up a very long black stocking at the foot of the bed, hoping Father Christmas would come and put something in it. I woke up Christmas morning and oh yes! there was something in my stocking. A new penny, an orange, a small box containing four chocolates, a pink sugar pig and some currants."

Then we would hear mother call up the stairs, 'Come along children we will be late for church'. There was a scramble down the stairs to see who could get there first to the one tap in the house for a wash. Father would say to the girls, 'You go first'. On everyone's plate on the breakfast table was a present: a pipe for father, a small bottle of perfume for mother, and each child got a story book according to our age. Then we set out over the fields to walk to church. Sometimes it would be snowing all the way there. It was a well-filled church and as father was the leader of the Young Men's Bible Class, he was well known. After Christmas greetings to our friends after the service, there was a long walk home and sometimes I had a ride on father's back. Back home mother would prepare the dinner.

"On Christmas Eve mother and father would have walked to Leeds Market. It was there that chickens were sold off for half-a-crown (12½p) each, so we were able to have a chicken on Christmas Day and Boxing Day for five shillings (25p). We had a large black fire oven to cook them in and there would be a huge pan of potatoes on the open fire. While mother was cooking the meal, father would light a fire in the small room in front of the house, which we called the parlour, and after dinner we would go in there. Father would go to sleep and we would have to be quiet and read our books. At 5 o'clock, mother would prepare tea: jelly and custard and one piece of cake each. Back in the warm parlour for the evening, we sang carols. I thought that we were very lucky as our house was the only one with a piano. It had two brass candlesticks on the front to hold the candles which lit up the music for mother to play. We also had an oil lamp hanging from the ceiling but this did not give much light.

"Mother's brother, Uncle Dan, who lived in Bramley village came along with his wife to help us sing. Father sang 'Silent Night' and we sang 'Away in a Manger'. The singing went on until 9 o'clock, then my sister and I had to go to bed. Mother prepared supper and my two older brothers were allowed to stay up and have supper with the adults. I thought how lucky they were. My aunt would come upstairs with us, hear our prayers, tuck us up in bed and blow out the candle. I would stay awake for a while thinking what a lucky little girl I was and what a nice Christmas Day it had been."

My grandfather had changed his name from Walling to Nelson when he moved to Leeds from Liverpool. His decision to take his mother's maiden name was thought to have been made when he changed his job and didn't wish – for some reason – his previous employers to know where he had gone. It caused some confusion in the family for many years afterwards. Uncle Will changed his name back to Walling when he married, but Auntie Nellie, who never married, and Dad kept the name of Nelson until 1939 when

Identity Cards and Ration Books were issued.

In spite of Dad's back problems, he served in France with the Royal Lincolnshire Regiment during the 1st World War, being called up under the 'Derby Scheme'. This scheme was originated by Lord Derby MP, while serving as Director General of recruitment. It began in 1915 as a voluntary system in a last attempt to obtain recruits for the armed services in sufficient numbers essential to maintain the conduct of the war. All men between the ages of 18 and 41 were invited to enlist. Those who did so were 'attested' and ranged into 46 different groups to be called up when required – single men first. It failed to attract sufficient numbers so it was decided to introduce compulsory military service.

Dad never talked about his experiences in France but with over 1 million dead and 2 million wounded during the conflict, it is not surprising that most men returning home left their memories behind. What is known is that a shell burst near a number of them while either stretcher-bearing or digging trenches and that he came home temporarily blinded, to recuperate in St. Luke's Hospital, Bradford.

Before going into the army however, Dad had had a job as a commercial traveller which led him to visit Cronk's factory in Leeds, where he fell in love with a girl who worked there packing men's and ladies' hats into boxes. She was only a young girl in her teens and very shy. When she wrote to him as a soldier, she addressed him as 'Dear Nelson', too embarrassed to use his Christian name. He said that he would marry her when she was twenty-one, so my mother and father were married on July 16 1921, seven days after my mother's 21st birthday. Following their wedding, they were driven to the railway station in an open carriage to catch the train to Bridlington where they spent their honeymoon.

Mother lived not far from Leeds city centre with her mother and father, four sisters and her brother, George. He also served in the army for a while towards the end of the war by lying about his age – he was under sixteen and a half years old when armistice was declared in November 1918. Her father, my grandpa, had fled from Germany to escape conscription in the Prussian Army in the middle of the 1890s. Born in the village of Riestedt, near Sangerhausen in Saxony, he had served his apprenticeship as a Rasir and Friseur – a barber. He was Richard Oswald Siebenhuner and he found lodgings with a Mr and Mrs Rolf (he was Danish and she German) in Earl Street, Finsbury Park, London. There he fell in love with their married daughter, Ottilia (Tilly) Banzameer who was three years older than my grandpa. Together they went to live in Brighton where mother's eldest sister, Rosa, was born in 1898. Returning to London, they lived in a number of places before eventually marrying, following her divorce from her first husband who had previously returned to his native country of Switzerland. During this time, mother, (Edith Florence) was next to be born in 1900, then George Edward two years later, both at Twickenham: Mabel Violet and Clare Marguerite at Richmond in 1904 and 1906, and finally Lily Martha at Finsbury Square in 1908. 'Tilly' also gave birth to a number of other children who did not survive.

Less than two years later in 1910, and after first taking the family to Nottingham to live and then back again to London, Grandpa found a house in Winfield Mount in Leeds. He had all their furniture, hardware and luggage sent by railway from their last London home at a cost of four pounds one shilling and a penny, on October 15th 1910. This house was my grandparents' home until grandma died in 1954 aged 83, and grandpa in 1960 aged 85. They were a loving and devoted couple, their secret of how they had started life together remaining with them until they died.

Because of his nationality, Grandpa was sent to York for interrogation at the beginning of the 1914-18 War but returned home. Soon afterwards he was taken to be interned in a camp for foreign nationals in the Isle of Man where he remained until the end of the war.

He was number 13856 and lived in Flat 5a, Camp 3, Compound

3, Knockaloe Alien Camp. Life was hard and food in short supply. It was said that they once killed a dog that roamed the camp and ate it. Returning home he decided to call himself Richard Oswald, dropping the name of Siebenhuner and from then on the family adopted Oswald as their surname. There was understandably, quite a strong anti-German feeling in this country during the First World War, due no doubt, to the heavy casualties being suffered in France, and life could not have been easy for the girls attending Blackman Lane School during the war years 1914-1918 with a German surname – but they were (after all) essentially an English family (grandma was born in London) even though they had a German father. During the Second World War in 1940 and immediately after Dunkirk, he was again taken for interrogation, this time to Leeds Town Hall. Remembering how long he had been kept waiting the last time at York, he took with him a pack of cards to idle away the time. However, after only a brief interview during which they learned that his son had been in the British Army during the First World War, he was released.

The house they lived in was the third from the end of a very long terrace. At the back of the house was a small walled yard containing a tiny toilet building, which was reached by going down three or four steps. A few strides across the yard from the cobbled street you arrived at the door which led straight into their warm and cosy living room. In the attic, which was at the top of a very narrow and steep flight of stairs from the second floor, was a bath and wash basin. However, the sink in the corner of the living room was more convenient for the quick wash. Next to it was a single gas ring, used among other things for grandpa's fried breakfast, but the cooking was done mainly on the black range heated by a coal fire. Milk and meats were kept at the top of the steps behind the cellar door, away from the warmth of the room. A door in the other corner led to the stairs and front room, furnished for grandpa's customers coming to have their hair cut. His clientele were often visited by him at their homes or places of work and sometimes he would be called for by a chauffeur-driven car sent by his customer. He would set off smartly dressed in a trilby hat, dark suit with a buttonhole, preferably a cornflower, with his raincoat over his arm and carrying a small brown leather case containing the tools of his trade. Before leaving he would spend a long time polishing his shoes. His customers loved him, and one once offered him a Christmas present of either a bottle of whisky or £1 note – they were about equivalent in those days. He thought for a while, looking first at the bottle and then the money. Finally he said, "I can't make up my mind; can I have zem both?" "For your cheek", said his customer, "you can" and he had the same two presents from him for many years afterwards.

He was full of stories and anecdotes and with his German accent they were much more colourful in the telling. He once told me that people said to him, "Mr Osvald, you're a poor advert for a hairdresser, vhy do you vear your hair so long?" (his hair was white in his latter years, was long around his ears and down the back of his neck and quite thin on top) "Vell you see, I vould tell zem, it is how silly you look ven you vant yours cutting!" He made his own haircream which was green and had the pleasant sweet smell of lavender. He told his customers as he tried to sell it to them, that it would stop their hair from falling out. "But what about you?" they would say "you have bald patches!" "Aha!" grandpa would reply, "you should have seen me when I was a young man, I vas completely bald!"

He had no understanding of sport and although my aunts were keen Yorkshire County Cricket fans, the 'Noblest Game' was a complete mystery to him. Rugby League Football was too, and he told me that once he had been walking by the Leeds Ground at Headingly when a match had been in progress. Hearing a roar from the crowd, he had gone in to see what was happening. "Vot ver you cheering for?" he asked. "It was a Try" he was told. "Only a try?"

queried my grandpa "vot sort of noise vill you make ven zey score?"

Grandpa always appeared to be enjoying his life and could be described as a very happy man. His joviality and pleasant personality endeared him to his customers. He once gave me a complimentary ticket – he had quite a few in his drawer – to visit the Odeon Cinema in Leeds and after I had explained who had given me the ticket, I was shown to a very good seat in the circle by the Manager. I was only about 14 years of age at the time, and when I told my grandpa how I had been given VIP treatment, he said, "Of course you had VIP treatment – the Manager knew that if he hadn't have looked after you, I vould have given him a bad haircut next time!"

He was never still and even into his 70s – when he was still working – he rarely sat down for any length of time. He enjoyed his suppers of German sausage, meats, pickles and cheese which he would buy from Leeds Market. Even when he was eating he would fidget, moving the salt and pepper pots to a dozen or more different places on the table as if playing a solo game of chess. In a kind of nervous twitch he would close his eyes tightly then re-open them immediately, smile at his thoughts, – move the salt pot to a new position – give a little chuckle then relate one of his many amusing stories.

He liked my father and always spoke well of him to me. Soon after the War ended on November 11th 1918, Dad returned to his previous employment, and five or six years later found that he was now travelling more and more for the firm of Wilson and Stafford in Atherstone, which brought him to the North Warwickshire Market Town on numerous occasions. He was offered a job to work in the hat factory on the staff as a warehouseman. With now a small family to support – my brother and sister had been born, and the family were living in rooms in Leeds with a Mr and Mrs Hulbert – the offer was a heaven-sent opportunity to leave a city with its soot and grime, and move into the country and bring up his family in a much more healthy environment. Dad lodged for a while with a Mr and Mrs Holt in Stafford Street until a new semi-detached house, that Wilson and Stafford were having built, was ready. The family moved in at Whitsun 1925. I was born almost three years later. Mr Holt, who also worked at the factory, was my godfather.

At this time, the family was still called Nelson, since Dad had not bothered to change to our correct name of Walling. He believed that had he done so, his new employers might have found it strange that he had suddenly altered his name immediately after coming to work for them.

Grandpa liked to tell the story about the only time that he visited Atherstone soon after I was born. He had travelled by train from Leeds City Station, now brightly lit with electric light, and changing to the lower level line at Tamworth noticed that the station had only gas-lamps.

"Vot vill happen ven I get to Atherstone?" he used to say "vill zey only have candles?"

My mother, I believe, was his favourite daughter, and although Dad had taken her over 100 miles away from him, grandpa was content in the knowledge that she was happily married and had settled into her new home in a small country town.

# CHAPTER THREE

# My Kind of Town

"Atherstone was believed to have been developed from a Saxon settlement. AEthelred's Tun, which was a crossing of the route from Derby and Ashby to Coleshill and Oxford with the Watling Street. Maybe at this point houses and hostelries appeared, to provide rest and refreshment for travellers. It could also have become a centre for the distribution of farm produce grown on the rich lands either side of the River Anker" – which on one side of Atherstone marked the county boundary between Warwickshire and Leicestershire.

"Tradesmen's inventories early in the 16th century have ample evidence for a thriving cloth and wool trade. A draper and a haberdasher were selling their goods at this time and at least two weavers were working. Numerous items of wool, flax and hemp suggest others in the same trade. During the 17th century many weavers' and tailors' goods were appraised and in the last decade of the century two felt makers, Thomas Wilday and Joseph Hatton, had established the basis for the 19th century hat trade, for which Atherstone became famous."

When Dad arrived, there were five Hat Factories in Atherstone one of which had originally been a tannery. What had started out as largely a cottage industry was now playing a major role in bringing employment to the town. It was still a common sight right up into the 1950's to see women carrying huge black bags of trilby hats in order to do the 'trimmings' in their homes. This entailed sewing both the narrow leather band which went inside the hat, and the silk band – with its bow – round the outside.

"Prior to the 18th century most of the Atherstone population was involved in agriculture, either directly or indirectly and by the end of the 16th century, as the traditional grain market continued to expand, people began to supplement their agricultural income by trading.

"The market catered for many different trades during the 17th century and its cleanliness and efficiency were assured by the officers of the Manor Court. The twice weekly market and the annual Statutes Fair in September still continue today but in a different form. The market which impressed Daniel Defoe as a great cheese trading centre has again reverted to a general market, but with few locally produced goods. The annual fair (which dates back to the 14th century) has lost its former role as a labour market and is now solely for entertainment."

With the demolition of the houses in Station Street in the 1930s, a ready-made site presented itself for the Statutes Fair. Stalls which had previously lined Long Street were now able to be closer to the roundabouts and side shows. The family outing to the 'statutes' was a treat to look forward to each September. Thousands of coloured lights transformed the area into a magic fairyland, and we rolled our pennies down wooden chutes and sat clinging to the twisted 'candystick' pole as we rode the "Horses" on the roundabout. We had a couple of turns on the 'Cakewalk', and perhaps a ride or two on the 'Dodgems'. We watched men throwing darts at playing cards, shooting at white tin ducks, and we dodged the hard wooden balls that were thrown at large coconuts which never seemed to fall off their pedestals. After Dad bought a bag of brandy-snap and a coconut to take home from one of the brightly-lit stalls, we'd had a wonderful evening.

At first our house in Coleshill Road was lit by gas as the first electricity supply didn't arrive in the town until 1922 and at the time was not readily available except for Long Street and the bottom end of Coleshill Road. Opposite the front of the house at the end of Stanley Road, was a small field, and at the bottom of the garden were also fields prior to the building of Stratford Avenue council estate.

"Until this time the physical development of Atherstone was still very much centred on Long Street, the Market Square and Coleshill Road. Long Street, which followed the line of the old Watling Street, had always been the centre of the town and consisted of large private houses, shops and the 'yards' where most of the working population lived. The yards consisted of a varying number of small houses. The accommodation was in most cases very limited and over-crowding was quite common, as there were often as many as ten people living in one house. In the older yards there was only one tap for the use of the whole yard, and a closet would be shared by many families.

"As can be seen, the ordinary population worked and lived hard but there were some pleasures to be found. Atherstone had always had more than its fair share of pubs, and the period covering the second half of the 19th century and some years into the 20th, was no exception. Many of the yards had their own pub and yard bearing the same name".

Slum clearance didn't start until 1930. The demolition of the yards off Long Street was accompanied by large areas of new council house building. However, it was well into the 1950's before most of the old houses were demolished and more housing built away from the town centre and at Mancetter.

The disappearance of these houses in Long Street brought to an end the beautiful decorated yard entrances which were created by the tenants for the Carnival. Garden Row with their display of flowers and greenery won first prize on numerous occasions for the best decorated yard. Preceding the Carnival the 'King' and his 'Courtiers' would select people to be 'Knighted – for a fee – from the crowds waiting on the pavement, followed by Mr Propert in clown's costume bouncing his blown-up pig's bladder of top of children's heads.

An annual tradition which still takes place in Atherstone is the Shrove Tuesday Ball Game. I am not aware of any changes that have taken place since I left the town in 1964 except that rules were introduced in the 1970s to prevent it from becoming a brawl. During the morning of this almost unique free-for-all event, shop windows were boarded up and at 3 o'clock in the afternoon, a specially made huge leather ball was flung from the window of the 'Blue Bell' pub, usually by a well known celebrity, to the crowd below, preceded by handfuls of new pennies being thrown out to the children. The first scramble (the children having made a hasty retreat) was for the red, white and blue ribbons fastened to the ball and the 'honour' of the first kick. After an hour or so of booting the ball up and down Long Street, Market Street and Church Street, the ball would then be burst and 'smuggled' by the roughest and toughest men of the town.

The precise origins of the Shrove Tuesday Ball Game are not known. Certainly the game has a long history. It was played in the Middle Ages and may even date back, as some believe, to the reign of King John and Atherstone is one of the few places where the mediaeval custom of Shrove Tuesday Football still survives.

The Cheshire family or the Russell brothers often 'won' the ball when I was a lad and the memory of a group of sweating bodies in a scrum, perhaps jammed tight in either an entry or one of the yard's wash-houses, smuggling the ball, remains clearly in my mind. Strangely it was very rare for someone to be badly injured, but damage to property often occurred. One amusing incident I remember clearly was when the ball burst after landing on the point of an iron railing. It was taken to Mr Johnson's leather shop who, incidentally had made the ball that year. After it was repaired and 'thrown out' to the crowd with great ceremony by Mr Johnson, someone carelessly kicked it straight through his unprotected upstairs window!

The police were always ready to try to protect property, and made great efforts while the ball was being smuggled to keep the scrum in the centre of the road and, with the help of the crowd, to keep them moving. What we most enjoyed was to see them forced along to the end of Long Street to where a bit of the old Watling Street – still cobbled – went under the railway known as the 'Cattle Arch'. It didn't then take long for the crowd to push them into the often icy waters of the canal, which quickly sorted out who had the ball!

The Coventry Canal, which passed through Atherstone, linked with the Birmingham to Fazeley Canal close to Tamworth. Although the canal wasn't as important as when it was used as a means of carrying clay, pottery and coal south through the Midlands, Barlows's coal-laden boats could often be seen coming through Atherstone. There were many locks between Fazeley and the Coleshill Road bridge which was a convenient place for the boats to stay overnight and give a rest to the lean horses that pulled them. Here also was the entrance to the 'Basin' and Minions Wharf, once the centre of trade in Atherstone prior to the arrival of the railways in the second half of the 19th century. At the wharf the flour-mill remained and lorries brought the grain and took away the flour in huge sacks. The slow rhythmic chugging of the machinery throbbed monotonously, and the pleasant dry, earthy and dusty smell of the flour contrasted sharply with the fumes of the Gas Works on the other side of the canal. Built in 1841, here you could purchase coke for greenhouses and lime for the garden.

Further down the road on the opposite side of the 'Basin' was the London, Midland and Scottish Railway line (LMS) which carried – in addition to the local trains and goods wagons – the London Euston to Glasgow expresses. On the way home from the nearby South Junior School, we would climb on to the wall to watch the trains down below as they emerged from under the bridge beneath Coleshill Road. It was a great thrill to see the new streamlined blue and silver 'Coronation Scot' hurtling along the track, or perhaps in the same 'Royal' series the identical engines of the 'King George V1', 'Queen Elizabeth', 'Princess Elizabeth' and the 'Princess Margaret Rose'.

Just over the steep canal bridge and built by the side of the canal was Wilson and Stafford's Hat Factory where Dad had come to work. Large crates were constructed in the factory workshop to contain the hats that would be going by train. These were then loaded on to a long horse-drawn dray and taken to the railway station. Later, the high entrance into the factory, allowed the tall green container lorries to reverse into the yard and to load up with the cardboard boxes, also full of hats that had been packed in Dad's department.

Further up the road, our house was not far from the entrance to the Outwoods, with farming country on the far side and the woods of the Merevale Estate to the right behind the great wall. The Outwoods may have been the land referred to in 'Dugdale's' "Warwickshire", when he says that the lands with which Robert Earl Ferrers endowed Merevale, included "all his Forest of Arden (i. e. his OUT-WOOD in that part of the Woodland which then bore the name of Arden)".

Although the area was common land where cattle and sheep had once grazed, it was now also a nine-hole golf course and barbed-wire fences still surrounded the greens to protect them from straying animals. The professional was a Mr Hunt whose two sons became nationally famous as golfers in later years after they had left the town, with Bernard captaining the Ryder Cup Team in 1973 and 1975.

During the summer when the ground was hard and slippery, and the grass burnt brown by the hot sun, the lids from Mother's cake tins were ideal for sitting on and sliding down the hills (as long as she didn't find out) but they never did quite fit afterwards.

In the winter we would use a home-made sledge on those same hills after it had snowed, and jump through the drifts – where the wind had used the snow to change the contours of the ground – only perhaps to land on a prickly gorse buried beneath its white camouflage.

When we were even younger, we would search in vain for the four-leafed clover or see who could make the longest daisy-chain before it fell apart, as we carefully made a slit in the soft, thin stalks with our thumb nail, and slid the next one through. Away from the fairway of the golf course, we had fun catching grasshoppers as they revealed their whereabouts with their loud chirping then, slowly opening our hands, watch as their green, brown or reddish bodies crouched on our palms ready to leap away two or three feet forward to be lost again in the long grass.

Using the winding paths that the sheep had made, we rode our imaginary horses over the 'Wild-West' 'double-mountains' and the 'puddin'-hill', then rested for a while on the way to 'the level' to lie in the warm sunshine, close perhaps to a harebell with its delicate blue flower ringing silently in the breeze at the top of its green slender stalk. As well as the golf course, the Outwoods was a place to exercise the dog, and where courting couples walked hand-in-hand or lay together in each other's arms, partly hidden in the little hollows between the fairways.

A little way further on past the Outwoods along the way to Ridge Lane was Monks Park Wood, known locally as the Bluebell Woods. This large area of broad-leafed woodland, with ivy thick on the trunks of trees, an abundance of insect life and numerous varieties of wild flowers, was a paradise for wild animals and birds. Beneath the trees grew large areas of bracken deeply rooted in the soft spongy leaf mould. The double-toothed petals of the creeping buttercup gave extra colour in the midst of the soft greens of the many varieties of ferns and mosses growing alongside a stream which meandered through a small valley in the wood. The pinkish-purple of the foxglove stood elegantly in the clearings, and in the height of the season we would walk off the wide footpath into the thick carpet of blue flowers to pick large bunches of bluebells – with their long green and white stalks – to take home (something which we would now be quite properly prosecuted for under the 1968 Countryside Act). During the late 1950's, open-cast coal mining devastated the centre of the wood. Although the land was later restored, contours had changed and the lovely ancient woodland was gone forever and the wildlife habitat destroyed.

Future generations will look back on our selfish attitude in the 20th century, when thousands of miles of hedgerow and vast acres of ancient woodland were destroyed, marshland drained, heathland lost for ever, all for the sake of a bit of coal, a new road or badly thought out urban development. The cost to the environment has been tremendous, in both lost species and numbers of varieties of all kinds of wildlife and flora, from that which was abundant at the end of the 19th century.

Fortunately a little of the woodland was left untouched and on the other side of Coleshill Road in Merevale Park, the picturesque setting of the thatched Bee-Hive cottage also remains. Mr and Mrs Heath resided there as long as I could remember and her bird table had many visitors, including members of the tit family, finches and the distinctive black, white and red Greater-spotted Woodpecker. She once told me that she had a robin that regularly tapped on her window asking to be fed.

A mile or so further up the road was the 'Horse and Jockey' inn, situated at one of the highest points in Warwickshire. The sign outside the inn was replaced in the 1950's after Sir William Dugdale's son rode Cloncarrig in the 1951 Grand National. When the artist came to paint the picture of him on that horse, the photographs were not very clear so he painted the sign with the jockey on another horse called Le Jacobin. However, as Cloncarrig was a brown and Le Jacobin was a French Bay colour, the artist ensured that the painting conformed to Cloncarrig's likeness by visiting the horse which was currently in retirement at Merevale. The future Sir William is depicted wearing his then racing colours of white with black sleeves and a rose cap. In 1970, his wife repainted the picture as the original had become damaged by condensation under the glass cover.

Opposite the inn, a path through the Bentley Woods came out in Ridge Lane conveniently close to another pub, and although this was a longer walk from the 'Horse and Jockey' back home, past the Bluebell Wood, Pitman's dairy farm and across the Outwoods, it was one I enjoyed taking.

Another country walk went across the field opposite the 'Blubell Wood' down to a wooden bridge over a little stream where we would stop for a while to play 'pooh-sticks'. The walk continued up the hill and came out into a lane which led to Mancetter. Here one could either take the route through the woods of Purley Chase then back across the Outwoods, or continue past the reservoir to Oldbury Hall. One could then walk across Hartshill Hayes, through Mr Bloor's fields to his farm, to return home via the canal tow-path. I can recall a Scout Camp in those fields when a member of the troop was sawing a dead branch off a tree. Luckily for him someone happen to notice that he was sitting on that same branch at the time and a warning shout prevented what might have been disastrous consequences! From Mr Bloor's top fields, one had excellent views of the Leicestershire countryside as far as the hills in Charnwood Forest. Nearby, a kestrel perhaps would be hovering, searching for a field vole on the ground below, or we might watch a hare dashing across the ploughed land, then stop abruptly to listen, ears pricked, and with a high kick, scamper towards a far-off hedge.

There would be skylarks ascending almost vertically to great heights, their positions revealed by their familiar trilling song.

There were many short walks for a Sunday afternoon or a summer evening; along Church Walk to the Vicarage then on to the 'Bathing Bridge' or, 'Lover's Walk' starting close to the 'Cattle Arch' alongside the allotments, and round to Gypsy Lane and into Sheepy Road. The Twenty-one Oaks walk, however, was perhaps the favourite, although I believe we talked about it more than we did it. When we were children, Dad often answered our cry of "What shall we do?" with, "Take a walk round the Twenty-one Oaks!" It was a road walk that skirted Merevale Park and approaching a small meadow opposite the old Toll-Gate cottage in Coleshill Road, we would clap our hands together to see the white bob-tails of the rabbits as they scampered back to their warrens. Continuing up the Rope-Walk hill and past the Beehive cottage, and then climbing the even steeper hill to the top lodge at the south entrance to Merevale Park, we could see the road with the twenty-one oaks lying ahead on the right. As we walked along it counting the trees as we passed by, we had a good view of the dark grey brickwork of Merevale Hall and a flag flying from the tower denoted that Sir William Dugdale was at home. We would now complete the circular walk by turning down Merevale Lane, (close to Baddesley Colliery), past Merevale Church and back to Atherstone. Here we could choose to use the tow path alongside the canal to Coleshill Road and home.

I've walked or cycled many miles along that tow path and have been met occasionally by a horse keeping close to the hedge with a tow rope to the barge preventing anyone from getting by. It wasn't the most pleasant experience to have to press against a hawthorn hedge, especially in short trousers, in order to allow the horse to pass and avoid being knocked into the 'cut' by the rope.

The 'bathing bridge' at the far side of the Outwoods, as its name implies, was a popular place for diving off and for swimming in that part of the canal. However, it wasn't as pleasant as it sounds. It was not uncommon to see, floating in the canal, bloated cats and dogs which had been purposely drowned by their owners.

It also took its toll in suicides and fatal accidents including 'Consul' Green (I've no idea why he was called 'Consul') who sold the 'Nuneaton Observer' on the streets announcing the newspaper in a sharp and brisk manner as the 'Obse'-ver'. He was found dead in the canal at Minions Wharf early one morning with his 'papers floating in the water and was thought to have walked in accidently in the fog the previous evening.

Mr Pond too, was found in the canal one morning after being reported missing. He had worked in the packing department at Wilson and Stafford's and was succeeded by Mr Ball, a close and lifelong friend of my father. If Dad was working late, I liked to take his tea down to him that mother had prepared – sandwiches and a home-made rock-cake perhaps and his tea in a bright blue enamelled can. I enjoyed chatting to Bill Herod in the carpenter's shop, watching Mr Ball packing the crates, or Elsie in Dad's department, neatly wrapping the hats in tissue-paper-lined oval-shaped cardboard boxes.

The days began with various hooters sounding around 8 o'clock calling the men and women to the hat factories. The men on the morning shift at Baddesley Colliery would have long gone but at lunch time they could be seen standing in a little group on the corner of Erdington Road and Coleshill Road, waiting for one of Evans's buses to take them to Baddesley Colliery for the afternoon ('married-man's) shift. Over their shoulders hung strong canvas bags inside which were their 'snap' tins containing the food they were to eat down the pit. Waiting to go to their work, they never looked as happy as my father going to his – which was naturally understandable – and I remember my father once told me that he heard one say to the other in a voice loud enough for my father to hear as he was returning to the factory on the opposite side of the road,

"Look at that little 'Tory', he doesn't know what it's like to work for a living".

I know my father voted Labour, Liberal and Conservative throughout his life but not necessarily in that order. However, possibly as a reason to remain neutral in a small town where everyone knew everyone else, he was a member of both the Miner's Welfare Club and the Conservative Club and at one time, the Liberal Club too!

Evans's Buses had a variety of passenger vehicles over the years and at one time had what was known as a 'horse-box' because of its peculiar shape. They had a regular service taking miners to their collieries and back. Fully laden they would laboriously and slowly climb the hills up Coleshill Road, the driver gradually working down through the gears until finally, now in its lowest gear, the engine would pull the vehicle to the top of the hill, take what appeared to be a deep breath and carry on with its journey.

The regular out of town bus was the Midland Red 765 service, which journeyed between Lichfield and Coventry. I used the service to go to and from Nuneaton regularly when I started work after leaving the Navy. It ran every hour but sometimes was full, and I often had to wait another hour for the next one to come along before I could get on. Once I remember walking back from Nuneaton one Christmas because all the buses were full.

I was encouraged, but not forced, to go to Sunday School from a young age. The classes were taken at South Junior School and sometimes we would walk from there in a long procession to the church for the morning service. The numbers were usually well depleted by the time we'd arrived as some 'disappeared' on route. We would be welcomed by the Rev. Manley who was Vicar at St. Mary's for as long as I can remember – he even officiated at my marriage in 1951. My mother called to him once as he was cycling over the canal bridge in Coleshill Road, to answer my typical child's question of "Where is God?" He raised his arms towards heaven and said, "Everywhere!" He could often be seen cycling around the town in his clerical-grey suit on his way to visit his parishioners, and on seeing one of his congregation would dismount, raise his hat, give a broad smile and with a "good morning" or "good afternoon", remount and continue on his way.

Another well known clergyman was the Rev. Owen, the Congregational Minister. He lived in 'The Manse', a house a few doors away from our house in Coleshill Road. Before the war he was Group Scout Master of the 1st Atherstone Scouts for a while and in the 1950's he left the Church to become Registrar – 'it was a much better paid job'- he once told me.

I remember the years before the war as those of stability and security. It wasn't the same for all families. Poverty was very evident from the way that some of the children were clothed and it was easy to recognise which children came from homes where a regular wage was earned by the 'breadwinner', and the mother, or 'housewife' was capable of managing the household finances. Most men, I believe, handed their wage packets to their wives, and after giving pocket money to their husbands and putting away the amounts required for the gas and electric meters, rent, rates, insurance, clothes and various other items, the rest went on food and household goods. Mother had a dark green 'Black Magic' tin in which she saved this money each week and the system seemed to work very well for her.

We bought a new wireless from Mr Large's shop (next to the Regal Cinema) in the 1930's and we'd listen to the bands of Jack Payne, Ambrose and Henry Hall, and Dad's favourite singer, Elsie Carlisle.

On a serious note, the siren would sound in the town at 11am on the 11th November each year to pronounce two minutes silence to be observed in memory of the millions of dead in the first World War, 1914-1918. However, when the Italians bombed and invaded Abbyssinia in 1935, we sang as children, and without any feelings of remorse,

"Won't you come to Abyssinia won't you come,
Bring your own ammunition and your gun,
Mussolini will be there throwing bombs up in the air,
Won't you come to Abyssinia won't you come".

# CHAPTER FOUR

# EARLY ROUNDS

I was born left-handed but forced to use my right at school: conformity was essential in the 1930's. As a result I developed a stammer which was very pronounced when I was young and I did not fully overcome it until about half-way through my working life. However, in spite of this speech impediment I was not shy and at my last school I was given the only speaking part in an oriental mimed 'No' play. Dressed in Japanese costume I began, "I am the Chorus and I am here to tell you about the play our actors are here to perform." I've forgotten what the play was about except that Frank Healey and Doreen Wilkinson sat in a 'boat' on the stage and later on, Leslie 'Bomber' Hall walked on with a basket scattering dead leaves across the stage as I stuttered, "It was Autumn time and the leaves were falling."

All outdoor sports activities had been stopped because of the war and, in any case, the playing fields were ploughed up later and planted with potatoes in the 'Dig for Victory' campaign. At the beginning of my second year, the school entered the Bird and Tree Competition organised by The Royal Society for the Protection of Birds. I chose to write about the thrush and the ash tree. We were all presented with a book entitled, 'The Story of Plants' which I still have. Almost 50 years later, I was to become an active member of the Society.

The reason I chose the ash and the thrush was simply because a song thrush often sang from the ash tree that Dad had planted at the bottom of the garden. From an early age I was able to recognise garden birds and both Mum and Dad fed them regularly. We had a fairly long but narrow garden most of which was laboriously dug each year and planted with vegetables. At the top of the garden nearest the house were pink and white rambler roses and a flower border, a small lawn and then, a little further down, a swing. I often used to sit on this to give my full repertoire of song, unaware of being a possible nuisance to the old lady who lived next door. One day she told me, in quite an unpleasant tone, to "shut up". I thought I'd better conclude my recital, which I did, with a verse of 'God Save the King' much to the amusement of my mother.

I suppose I was a bit mischievous and on occasions in the morning, I would dress very quickly, get out of the bedroom window, 'tightrope' the narrow metal bar across the rain water tank and climb down the coal-house door. I would then knock on the kitchen door, surprising my mother who moments earlier had seen me in bed. However, I wasn't fully responsible for our toffee-making disaster. Ron had assembled the ingredients and we left them on the gas stove to boil, not aware that it had to be watched very carefully and stirred. Soon it was solid, burnt black and stuck to the saucepan. In order not to be found out, we buried the lot in the garden, pan and all!

Perhaps mother was pleased when I at last joined the cubs but she was not particularly pleased when I came home from my first camp minus my vest. We had slept in a barn over the cow shed at Mr Carr's farm at Pinwall and I concluded that my undergarment had fallen through the gaps in the floor and been eaten by a cow below. When mother discovered that (added to this) we had bathed nude in the duck pond and been squirted with milk by the farmer as we watched him milk the cows, she was not amused. Fortunately I was allowed to remain in the organisation and following our successful surveillance over the Coronation bon-fire in 1937, we were rewarded in July that year, by attending the Leicester Rally and very lucky to get within touching distance of Lord Baden-Powell, the Movement's founder. A month later he made his last public appearance at the 5th World Scout Jamboree in Holland. It was held at Vogelensang and from all over the world came the members of the great family of Scouting. They gathered together from five continents. Britain created a new record by sending 8,000 boys which included a scout from the 1st Atherstone, Reg Croxall. Soon after the Jamboree, B-P retired to Kenya where he died $3^1/_2$ years later in January 1941, just before his 84th birthday.

In January 1939 when I was 11 years old I moved up into the Scouts, still in the 2nd Atherstone, joining the Owl Patrol. Later that year fifteen of us, including the two Scoutmasters of both troops, attended the Warwickshire County Rally, camping at Berkswell, near Coventry. My brother Ron, who was in the 1st Atherstone troop, also attended and the event was visited by the new Chief Scout, Lord Summers. Although the combined troops came third in the Camping Competition, what should have been a happy event was spoiled by my getting into a fight with Ernie Tooth over carrying water. We were both sternly reprimanded by our Scoutmaster, Bill Wykes, who reminded us both that not only had we broken the 4th Scout Law (A Scout is a friend to all etc. , ) but we had let down the troop in front of the whole county. It did the trick and we were always friends after that and eventually I became Patrol Leader of my own patrol, the Owls. Bill Wykes went into the army in 1940 and the two troops joined together under the 1st Atherstone Scoutmaster, Ray Pickering, who was Bill's brother-in-law. In spite of the war things went on as normal, at least as far as we were concerned, having summer camps at local farms, one as far as

Stoneleigh, outside Coventry, on a site which years later was to become the headquarters for the Royal Show.

Sometime before the war I had been given my first gramophone by my parents' friends, Mr and Mrs Cooper. Their only son, Donald, served in the 8th Army and was killed in the Desert Campaigns in North Africa. I was thrilled as I walked home later that evening carrying the black portable gramophone together with a few records I had been given. In Long Street I was looked at attentively by a policeman from across the road and Dad suggested jokingly, that perhaps he thought that I was a member of the IRA and carrying a bomb.

The IRA had in fact been active for some time and just before the start of the war, a bomb in a bicycle carrier, parked in Broadgate shopping street in Coventry, had exploded killing five people and injuring many more. The police arrested three men all claiming to be IRA loyalists, two of them being hanged in February 1940.

I was only vaguely aware of the trouble with the IRA at the time but I wouldn't have minded if the policeman had asked me to show him what I was carrying. He might even have enjoyed listening to my records of Sidney Custard playing "How High the Moon" on his saxophone or Frank Crummett singing "The Song of the Prune".

When I was 12, I took a job delivering morning newspapers for Baxters in Market Street. I was paid four shillings a week. The shop had only two 'rounds' one of which was fairly well scattered. George Cope did one and I the other and whoever got to the shop first in the morning had the choice. One bicycle was available and usually reserved for the longer round. At that time, there was a great distinction between the social classes and this was reflected by the type of newspaper delivered to the various homes. As a general rule the 'working classes' had the 'Daily Herald' and the 'Daily Mirror', the business man the 'News Chronicle' and the 'Manchester Guardian' and the professional classes the 'Daily Telegraph' and the 'Times'. I also delivered one 'Financial Times' to a solicitor.

The 'Daily Express and the 'Daily Mail' appeared to be read by all sections of the community.

Less than a year later I left Baxters (never really got used to those very early mornings) to be delivery boy for Collins' grocery store and on Saturday and school holidays I was an assistant in the shop. It was a family business started by the then present owner's father in about 1900. On entering the shop, one was immediately aware of the fragrance of mixed spices and dried fruit mingling with the aroma of freshly ground coffee.

The shop was double-fronted with the door in the centre. Wooden shutters were put up against the windows and an iron gate fastened and locked in front of the door when the shop was closed. As one entered, there was a dark wooden polished counter to the right with a coffee-bean grinder at the far end. On the opposite side of the shop were the dairy products. A hand-operated bacon-slicer at one end was next to the butter-board. The butter came in bulk and we cut and weighed it as required. The cheeses were also cut up on the counter. Sugar came in large sacks and as with all the products had to be carefully weighed, being already rationed due to the war. Tea came loose in silver-paper-lined tea-chests, and biscuits in tin boxes. Most things had to be packeted before being sold to customers, so there was always some work to be done. The mouth-watering smells of the dairy products and cooked meats blended with the fresh fragrances of tea and coffee and, although there was rationing, a little taste of cheese on a thinly-buttered cream cracker was hard to resist on occasions. Dried fruit had all but disappeared and by the time I left the shop in May 1942 – just after I left school – tinned fruit was put on 'points' and food rationing covered a hundred items.

Ration books were issued to everyone in January 1940, and rations varied throughout the war years according to supply. Sweets and certain foodstuffs were dealt with by 'points' rationing: a tin of luncheon meat for instance, being 16 points, a packet of biscuits or cereals, 4 points, and canned fruit, 8. As each ration book contained the same number of coupons to be used over a given period, a fair distribution of all the essential foodstuffs was ensured, and the 'points' system enabled people to have a certain amount of choice.

Although most people came to the shop, there were still deliveries to be made, mainly to the type of customer who read the 'Daily Telegraph' and the 'Times'! We rarely saw these people in the shop as they telephoned their orders in, direct to Mr Collins who, in addition to being a successful grocer, was well known for his musical abilities. As well as choir master and organist at St. Mary's Church, he was the Musical Director for the Coleshill Operatic Society of which many Atherstone people were members. When Atherstone Operatic Society was reformed in 1964, having been disbanded when the 'talkies' came to 'The Picturedrome' in the 1920's, Cyril Collins became Musical Director to that society also. I was on the committee of the newly formed group and in its first two years took on the role of Business Manager.

Now, however, twenty three years before that as a 13 year old, I had to concentrate on keeping my balance on an old heavy cycle piled high with baskets on the front, as Mr Collins watched me wobble away, fearful that I might spill all his precious provisions all over the road. I never did, but when the bicycle was fully laden it was a little difficult to control. The wide tubular steel framework over the front wheel held three or four wicker baskets – one inside the other – containing the groceries to be delivered to the different customers. It was most important to stack them in the right order for unloading purposes. On Saturday evenings after we had locked up, the two full time assistants and I would stand in the shop, waiting to be called in order of seniority, to go to the office behind the high 'walk-in' 'fridge to receive our wages. "LESLIE" – "REYNOLDS" – and finally "WALLING". I think the most I ever received was £1 when I worked during the school holidays, but talking and dealing with people, and also doing a little selling, was good training and prepared me for the type of work I was to do later when I came out of the forces.

Back in early 1940, Wilson and Stafford's found that demand for men's trilby hats had rapidly declined due to the number of servicemen, and this put their workforce on short time. Although Dad wasn't affected being a member of the staff and on a regular wage, he left the hat factory to work as a storeman at the Alvis Works in Coundon, Coventry, which was now making armoured vehicles instead of sports cars. On the night of 14 November 1940, Dad didn't come home and it wasn't until the next day – when he eventually arrived – that we learned that much of the centre of Coventry, including the Cathedral, had been destroyed in an air raid the previous night. We were aware, of course, that Coventry had been bombed being only 12 miles or so away but had not realised the extent. Picking his way over the rubble, Dad had been particularly saddened by the number of dead animals he had seen. In the all-night concentrated bombing, the number of casualties was high but in spite of this the people didn't lose their sense of humour. People thought it funny that the Rex cinema which had been showing the film 'Gone With the Wind' was destroyed. Shopkeepers who had no windows left had notices proclaiming that they were 'Still Open – more open than usual'. The Alvis Works had been hit a number of times but thankfully Dad had escaped unhurt.

Although spirits remained high, and defeat in the war unthinkable, the Axis powers were everywhere on the offensive and, from early 1940 until the autumn of 1942 there seemed to be no prospect of ending their advance. Pearl Harbour had been attacked by Japan in December 1941, bringing the United States of America into the war, but the Japanese had advanced so far south in the Pacific Ocean, that by the Autumn of 1942 they were threatening to descend upon Australia.

In Russia the Germans had reached the Caucasus oilfields and were at the gates of Stalingrad. In North Africa Rommel had reached El-Alamein and was only 60 miles from Alexandria and the German Luftwaffe controlled the air space over the Mediterranean, preventing all but a few Allied ships getting through to Malta. The U-boats in the North Atlantic were also having considerable success as all along the Atlantic Seaboard of North America, and in the Caribbean nearly all the shipping routes were sealed off. However, in May of this year, the first thousand-bomber raid took place on Cologne, followed by attacks on Essen and the Ruhr. In August, the American 8th Air Force also started their operations from Britain. It was in this atmosphere and exactly at this time that I left scouting and joined the 1162 (Anker)Squadron of the Air Training Corps (ATC).

One of the most enjoyable activities at the ATC was to belong to the Air Rifle Team. The Home Guard, the Fire Service, the Police and other war time groups all had teams playing one another on a weekly basis. I managed to keep my place in the team for a while and enjoyed competing against the Auxiliary Fire Service because they had my boss, Ken Ireland, on their team. He and his father, W. L. Ireland, were the Manager and Managing Director of Mancetter Granite Quarries Ltd. , where I now worked.

When I left school at Easter 1942, I also left Collins' shop and joined my brother in the office at the quarry as a clerk. We were the only office staff and shared a building with the M. D. and his son, the Quarry Manager. Although all the buildings and even the men who worked on the machine plant got covered in a thick grey dust, the office building situated on a hill side kept fairly clear. The granite which came to the crushing plant from the quarry in wooden wagons – pulled by horses – on a narrow-gauge railway line, was fed into the jaws of the machinery by hand. The stone was then screened into various sizes, and at another plant nearby most of it was covered by tar or bitumen and the finished product used for road surfacing or airfield runways. About 40 men worked at the quarry including one whose full-time job was looking after the horses, and two others who worked in the blacksmith's shop. I found it fascinating to watch them make horseshoes on the anvil and remember the heat from the fire and the pungent smell as the hot shoe was fitted to the hoof of the horse. The foreman was a quiet unobtrusive little man who would sometimes walk in the office with gelignite in his pocket. An expert with explosives, he appeared to be unaware of any danger handling detonators but always knew exactly what he was doing. He often appeared to be everywhere at once, one minute in the office and the next minute telephoning in from one of the quarry 'pits'. Sometimes he couldn't be found, and then he'd be seen walking from the Magazine (a small well-secured building in the middle of a field) with his bag of gelignite or lighting his fuses in the quarry and blowing his little bugle to warn everyone to take cover. Moments later a large section of the face in one of the pits would come crashing down in a cloud of dust, or perhaps he would run a series of controlled explosives (pops) to break up the huge boulders.

Twenty-four Italian POWs (Prisoners of War) from Maxstoke Park near Coleshill came to work at the quarry for a while but they were not suited to the heavy work. They were replaced by German POWs from the Camp at the Atherstone end of Merevale Park who, in contrast to the Italians, really tackled the job. At first they struggled with the heavy long-handled hammers trying to break the hard granite, but when they had earned respect from the experienced quarrymen, they were shown how to split the stone down the grain and that it wasn't necessary to use brute force. My brother, Ron, sometimes shared the task of ferrying the men to their respective camps in the Bedford truck and I occasionally went with Mr Ireland to Adcock's bakery in the town to fetch the hot meat pies which we gave free to the POWs as a reward for their work. Cash payments were not allowed, of course, but sometimes they were also given cigarettes.

Considering the high risk of injury due to the type of work being done at the quarry, it was remarkable that there was only one serious accident while I was there. Old Oliver Paxton who was in his 70's, sadly lost a leg and seriously damaged the other when one runaway steel wagon pinned him against another and he died a few weeks later. He was a Gloucestershire man with a rich West Country accent and lived next door to us with his two unmarried daughters. It was a tragic way for such a wonderful old man to lose his life.

I never took home more than £2 per week but I learned to use a typewriter, reply to correspondence (Mr Ireland occasionally put only one word across a letter that needed answering!) book-keep and deal in every way with the telephone switchboard. Every call out of town, in those days, was made through the telephone operator. Ron did all the more difficult work and the complicated calculations of the men's wages.

During this time I was studying for my National Certificate on a one day a week basis and also learning a lot of interesting subjects in the ATC. George Kimber, one of the quarrymen, and Mr Devy, manager of Cleelands Shoe shop in town, were the instructors in morse signalling and taught us well. They had both been in the Army Signal Corps and we sat round a long table, each of us with earphones and a morse key, and they taught us how to send messages to each other. At airfields we learned how to use a parachute by being fastened to a harness and spring-loaded cable, then jumping from a high platform inside a hanger. We also learned how pilots were taught to fly in the simulated cock-pit of the Link Trainer. I did fairly well, even if my approach on landing was a bit steep and wobbly but forgot to check my altimeter and landed a few feet below ground!

We had an old Avro Anson twin engined aircraft in the grounds of Grendon Lodge opposite the railway station, which was the home of Charles Vero and his family, another hat manufacturer in the town and also a pilot officer in the ATC. We also used the room above the garages for instruction purposes. Prior to this, subjects such as Navigation and Meteorology were taught at the Queen Elizabeth Grammar School in the classrooms – so I managed to get some education at that place after all!

# CHAPTER FIVE

# THE WAR YEARS

The six years between September 3rd 1939 and August 15th 1945 were times that we of our generation would never forget. I was luckier than a lot of young people of my age group, and in different parts of the country others had some terrible experiences.

Atherstone escaped any serious hardship during the war except, of course, those families whose loved ones had either been killed in the forces, or Coventry and Nuneaton air-raids, or who had been taken prisoner. It seemed to be a very safe place to live and many children were evacuated from the Coventry area to Atherstone and district. Whole families found refuge and relative peace there after being bombed out of their homes, and efforts were made by the people of Atherstone to accommodate them until they could return home.

Mum was always ready to help when asked and we first had a Mrs Liggins and her daughter Margaret living with us for a while. It didn't work too well especially as two women shared the one kitchen and there was the inevitable clash of personalities, but we managed. Margaret was close to her mother and both were visibly affected by what had happened to them in the air-raids. After Mrs Liggins and her daughter left, Alma came to stay with us. She was a little older than me and her family had been bombed out of their house in Foleshill on the outskirts of Coventry. She only stayed for a while before rejoining her family elsewhere.

Finally, Eileen Harvey was evacuated to us and stayed for about 3 years. She was one of the Stoke Park girls and about my own age. She was very self-assured, had a strong personality and was very independent. Although we got on quite well with each other, she wasn't my type – but some of her school-mates were! A few boys' hearts missed a beat when they passed the Coventry girls walking in the opposite direction towards the Grammar School. They were certainly a lot better looking than the girls from Atherstone, or we thought so at the time. I was the only one in my class at school to have at home an evacuee from either Stoke Park or Barrs Hill and when on a couple of occasions I had an invitation from Eileen to go to one of their school parties and take a friend, I was suddenly the most popular lad in the class.

I never succeeded in dating the best of the girls, although I tried, but they preferred the Grammar School lads. Eileen persuaded me to go out with one of the girls called Beryl, whose surname was Fowler. Naturally, her nickname was 'chucky' (chucky-fowl!) and she was quite fat. When I unkindly told her so, she said that she wasn't fat – only a little plump! She didn't want to go out with me again and I wasn't surprised! In addition to the schoolchildren who were evacuated to the town, a number of soldiers were stationed in Merevale Park. The grounds had always been kept private except for an area at the Watling Street end, where Sir William Dugdale had allowed the annual Flower and Agricultural Show to take place. We would walk to the park and go under the Cattle Arch railway bridge, looking at all the stalls of the vendors at the side of the road and pass the 'King's Head' public house where Stanley Holloway's mobile theatre often came to visit the town. As well as the usual monologue recitations the Company would put on melodramas such as 'Maria Martin' ('Murder in the Red Barn'). We used to enter the park along with hundreds of others, through the main lodge gates to the area where the Show was held. In those late pre-war summer evenings, a magnificent firework display lit up the night sky to cries of delight from the large crowd. It was spectacular and the event had been something to look forward to each year. The war put an end to all of this and a small part of the park became a transit camp for army units.

For the final year or so of the war, rolls of barbed wire were placed on top of the high wall which ran along the side of the park and the place became a German Prisoner of War Camp, from where we had the volunteers to work at the quarry. The prisoners were guarded by soldiers of the Polish Army. Prior to that a United States Army Unit had been stationed there and for a short while, 'The King's Own Scottish Borderers', and it was Eddie, from that Scots' Regiment whom we invited to our house on occasions, who introduced me to my first haggis. As a Scotsman he was anxious that we should try his National dish, but whether it contained all the ingredients during those days of shortages was extremely doubtful. The minced heart and liver would have been difficult enough to obtain, and the lemon juice and nutmeg virtually impossible. Nevertheless, we were told that it was the 'genuine article' and we all enjoyed it as I recall.

In addition to the soldiers who came to the Park, we also had members of the Women's Land Army who were housed in specially constructed huts built at Dowse's Nurseries in Witherley Road. The Women's Land Army trained and placed women in farm work and market gardening, and the girls in their uniform of green jersey and khaki breeches, helped on local farms and nurseries in an effort to produce more food.

The first soldiers to come to the park were a contingent of the Bedfordshire and Hertfordshire Regiment. Some brokenhearted girls were left in Atherstone when, towards the end of 1941, they left to join their comrades (less two companies) to help to reinforce the 1st Malaya Brigade in the defence of Singapore. It was a lost cause, and the defence was short lived, ending soon after they arrived. When the Japanese swept through the Malay Peninsula, there was little hope that Singapore would not fall quickly but in spite of the enemy being in sight of the port, stubborn fighting at the Pasir Panjang ridge resulted in the 1st Malay Brigade capturing this important Gap on the south-west section of the perimeter, on the 13th February 1942.

Next day, the Japanese army launched a heavy attack at 8.30am. supported by intense mortar and artillery fire on the front held by the Brigade. This and a number of other attacks were beaten off in bitter hand-to-hand fighting with severe losses on both sides. Early on the 15th, the 1st Malaya Brigade (which would have included the Beds' and Herts') withdrew, losing the Alexandra depot area with the remaining services of ammunition and stores. With similar situations being experienced by every Division, General Percival with his Chief of Staff met the Japanese Commanders and signed the terms of the surrender of Singapore.

For the way they had fought, the official records of the Bedfordshire and Hertfordshire Regiment show that they earned 'Accredited Battle Honours – Singapore Island – Malaya 1942'. The survivors of the Allied armies were to remain as prisoners of war for the next three and a half years.

The BBC also played a very important part in our lives during the war years and it wasn't until many years afterwards that it was revealed that a lot of discussion had taken place on what would be the best role for 'Auntie BBC'- as it was affectionally known – to play in times of war. Some wanted to meet the tastes of factory workers, others thought they knew what the forces would like to hear, and some wanted a much more serious approach to what was broadcast. Fortunately the 'entertainers' won, and we had "Music While You Work" during the day, and "Workers' Playtime" before the 1 o'clock News.

This programme at lunchtime was usually broadcast from "a factory somewhere in England" and included comedians Max Miller (the Cheeky Chappie), Vic Oliver, and Rob Wilton ("The Day War Broke Out"), comediennes Suzette Tarry and Beryl Ord and 'forces favourite' singers Vera Lynn and Ann Shelton. There were also The Western Brothers ('Play the game you cads, play the game'), Turner Leyton and Hutch, both singers at the piano, duettists Ann Ziegler and Webster Booth, Flanagan and Allen and the inimitable George Formby with his ukelele. There were many others.

Tommy Handley's ITMA (It's That Man Again), however, became the flagship of BBC wartime variety. ITMA characters made fun of people who wanted a more serious type of programme policy, with 'The Ministry of Aggravation', Colonel Chinstrap ("I don't mind if I do"), Sam Scram's "After you Claude – No after you Cecil" and, best of all, "Can I do you now sir?" from Mrs Mopp. In the evening we had more comedy and entertainment with 'Monday Night at Seven' (later to become Monday Night at Eight) and 'Band Wagon' with Arthur Askey and Richard 'Stinker' Murdoch.

We listened to more informative programmes such as "The Radio Doctor" telling us how to prepare our food to prevent us from getting stomach upsets and to eat more fresh vegetables, and then Mr Middleton, in a Sunday afternoon programme that was listened to by millions called 'In Your Garden', would tell us how to grow them. Mr Middleton once told us ". . . . beetroot is one of the most important war time vegetables because it ranks high in food value and we don't make enough of this excellent vegetable". Voices on the 'wireless' became people that we knew and looked forward to listening to. "Children's Hour" with 'Uncle Mac' included a programme "Out with Romany", perhaps the most famous and dearly loved children's programme ever broadcast. Romany, or in real life G. Bramwell Evens with his companions Doris (Gamble) and Muriel (Levy) and always with his dog Raq, would ramble through a wood or by a stream and describe what they saw, making the picture he painted in our minds come alive. We believed it, too, even though at that very moment through our windows, we could see the pitch black of a winter's evening.

Then for a different kind of humour we would occasionally tune in to 'Lord Haw Haw' on the 31 meter waveband. He broadcast from Bremen in Germany in English almost daily throughout the war, in an attempt to undermine the morale of the British people by spreading often false information and rumour. He once said that the British 'Minister of Misinformation' (!) had been conducting a systematic campaign of frightening women and girls about the dangers of being injured by splinters from German bombs. He went on to say that the women had reacted to these suggestions and alarms, by requesting their milliners to shape their Spring and Summer hats out of very thin tin plate, which was then covered by silk, velvet or other draping material!

His propaganda was, of course, never taken seriously and he became an object of derision. His real name was William Joyce – son of a naturalized Irish-born American – born in New York. He carried on fascist activity in the UK as a 'British subject', before going to Germany as a German-Nazi radio propagandist, making his last broadcast on April 30th 1945. He was captured, tried at the Central Criminal Court, London, on a charge of high treason, found guilty, and hanged on 3rd January 1946.

The bands we listened to on the wireless which brought so much pleasure during the war years included The Squadronnaires, The Skyrockets and the British Band of the AEF. I enjoyed listening to these but some of the older boys in the ATC introduced me to the even more popular bands of the USA. As records of these were more readily available now that the American forces were in this country, I soon became familiar with the different sounds and styles of Duke Ellington, Benny Goodman, Harry James, Jimmy Dorsey, Tommy Dorsey and, of course, Glenn Miller. As young teenagers we were keen cinema-goers and were able to see some of our favourite bands on the screen. We knew all the film stars, and the songs of the young Frank Sinatra and Bing Crosby. I once owned 50 records of Bing.

In contrast to all this, we danced in a small crowded room in the Town Hall, Market Street, to Stan Green and his band and drank pop at the interval. Stan was a newsagent in Long Street and an accomplished musician and played all the wind instruments, usually the alto-saxophone, bass-sax' and clarinet. He was accompanied by Jack on the piano, David on the double-bass and Atherstone's answer to Gene Kruper, Charlie, on the 'drums'. It became our regular Saturday evening get-together and I made a lot of new friends. Occasionally we danced in a much more sedate manner in the Grammar School Hall to Victor Sylvester records, learning the basic steps of the waltz, quickstep and slow foxtrot, under the watchful eyes of Maisie and Bill Hood.

Meanwhile the war went on and in 1943 there was a dramatic turn of events in favour of the Allies. In May of that year the 8th Army defeated the Germans and Italians in North Africa and in July the Allies invaded Sicily. By the beginning of September, when the Italian mainland had also been invaded, Italy surrendered. On the Russian Front the German army was being beaten both by the severe weather conditions and the firm resolve of the Russian fighting force. In the final six months of the year they had caused the Germans to retreat almost 300 miles in places and back into Poland. Successes were also being achieved by the Allies against the Japanese on the 'Forgotten Front' in Burma, and Australian and US troops were landing on the enemy-held islands in the Pacific with great success.

I never had any doubts that we would eventually defeat the Axis powers and the inevitability of the Allies invading the European mainland and freeing the German-occupied countries of France and the Netherlands, and subsequently Scandinavia, was eagerly awaited.

Then on the morning of June 6th 1944 we heard on the wireless the voice of John Snagge announce that "D-Day has come -" He went on to say, "Early this morning, the Allies began the assault on the north-western face of Hitler's European fortress." Later in the day, Richard Dimbleby, a BBC war correspondent who later was to become the finest commentator for the BBC, especially on state occasions, spoke to us from the front line. He reassured us with, "The British, Canadian and American troops who landed on the coast of France north of the lovely town of Caen, in broad daylight this morning, are already several miles inland on a front sufficiently broad to be more than a bridgehead -." There were to be eleven more months of hard fighting before Hitler was defeated.

When victory came on 7 May 1945, I was told, along with two of my friends, as we came out of the cinema late that evening. We made a quick dash to 'The Dolphin' to drink three pints before closing time as a prelude to the celebrations which were to start next morning on VE Day. Again we tuned in to the Home Service on the wireless, this time to listen to our Prime Minister, Winston Churchill, who had inspired us all throughout the war with his memorable speeches and now at last was telling us, "Yesterday morning at 2. 41am at General Eisenhower's Headquarters, General Jodl, the representative of the German High Command and Grand Admiral Doenitz, the Designated Head of the German State, signed the act of unconditional surrender of all German Land, Sea and Air Forces in Europe, to the Allied Expeditionary Force." Almost exactly three months later, and following the dropping of the first Atom bomb on Hiroshima and a second on Nagasaki, Japan also surrendered.

After VE (Victory in Europe) Day, some of the American GIs returned to marry the Atherstone girls they'd met previously. In addition to the one or two soldiers we'd invited into our home during the years, we also had two surprise visits from servicemen.

The Hulberts, whom Mum and Dad lived with in Leeds when they were first married, had a son Terry. He came to see us in his RAF uniform but the big surprise was when Dad's cousin from Australia, Herbert Ladd, paid us a visit. He was a huge man and looked very impressive in his army uniform and bush hat. He was well remembered by my father as 'little Herbert' but as he now towered above Dad by almost two feet as they shook hands; it was big Herbert greeting little Bert.

Life had changed dramatically from 1939 to 1945, not only for me but for all of us. It wasn't just that we were six years older but that everything we had been used to before the war had gone. Although we now had peace, it would be a long time before the politicians had sorted out the tangled mess of Europe or the end to shortages and food rationing but there was at last a future for people and a better life to live.

I just had two years in the Navy to look forward to and after a month thought that I'd like to sign on for seven years. After two months I began to wonder why I'd joined!

# CHAPTER SIX

# NAVY DAYS

We were a small group of 17-year-olds standing on Euston underground station waiting for the tube train to Waterloo, young men who had all volunteered to serve in the Royal Naval Air Service (RNAS) and leaving home for the first time. Nine of us had been to London previously and after watching two trains go by, we were approached by an inquisitive porter who asked, "What are you lads waiting for?" I had been put in charge of the party and had so far managed to get then to this point without mishap. . Taking on my responsibilities as leader and pointing to the indicator board above the platform replied confidently, "The train to Waterloo". "They all go to Waterloo", he said.

It was on the 14th August 1945 that we arrived at HMS 'Royal Arthur' at Skegness and were shown to our chalets, which had housed the holiday-makers before the war. Later in the day we learnt that Japan had surrendered. Following intensive bombing of twelve Japanese cities by B29s of the United States Air Force during the first week in August, the first atomic bomb was dropped on Hiroshima on the 6th. That date became a landmark in the history of mankind. Three days later, a second bomb was dropped, this time on Nagasaki, which prompted Japan to surrender. The 15th August was declared VJ (Victory over Japan) Day and the free world celebrated. Meanwhile we were refused leave to go into Skegness because we had no uniform, and we were not allowed to buy a drink of beer in the NAAFI as everyone knew that we were under the age of 18. So we drank a cup of tea and toasted the Allies.

At the end of the month, I joined other new recruits at one of the five 'HMS Gosling' camps near Warrington, for our twelve weeks' training. We learnt how to obey orders no matter how irrelevant. This was called discipline and was taught to us among other things, by our Maltese instructor, whom although only a Killick (Leading Seaman) we had to address as 'Sir'. However, he was very good and fairminded but naturally very strict. He taught us how to use the Lee-Enfield rifle and told us to treat them like we would our girl friends – to love and cherish , hold them tight and take great care of them. We realised the importance of this advice when we came to loading them with the . 303 ammunition and firing from the shoulder. If you didn't hold the rifle tight it could give you an unpleasant 'kick' and possibly a nasty bruise to follow. With the 'pig-sticker' attached, we learnt how to stick the short round bayonet into the enemy, which fortunately for us were bags of straw hanging on posts. We also did 'field-exercises'. These consisted of running over muddy fields dressed only in blue overalls and wearing plimsoles, crawling under barbed-wire fencing and lying face down in a bog as fire-crackers exploded all around us. What this had to do with servicing 'planes on aircraft carriers, I never did find out.

It was done no doubt, to turn us into fit men and a fighting force to be reckoned with. Apparently, the Admiralty had not told the training teams in the 'Gosling camps' that the war was over. We were certainly aware of it as we marched through the streets of Manchester in the Victory Parade. With our rifles at 'the slope', we were cheered as heroes by the large crowds lining the pavements.

In the Parade there were hundreds of soldiers, sailors and airforce personnel, who had all seen service during the war. Our youthful appearance together with the 'HMS GOSLING' on our hat-bands must have left no doubt that we were only new recruits under training but nevertheless, we were cheered just as loudly as the others.

We left the 'Gosling Camps' in November to go to the RAF Station at St. Athan in South Wales to be taught our various trades. After 5 months of instruction on the 9 cylinder radial and the 12 cylinder 'V' engines, I qualified as Air Mechanic (Engines) in April 1946.

On one memorable occasion while we were at St. Athan, an RAF Officer, Frank Whittle, came to the cinema on the camp to talk to us about how he had been the first person to apply the principle of jet propulsion to aircraft. He told us that the first jet aircraft had actually flown in 1941 and went on to give us an illustrated talk with the aid of a blackboard, on how the engine worked. After explaining the simple basic principles of the jet engine he concluded with, "All we now need is a spark to start the thing off with." We all gasped with disbelief at the apparent simplicity of it all, especially as we had spent months learning about the complicated workings of the internal combustion engine. For his work, Frank Whittle was Knighted in 1948 and given a government award of £100, 000 together with the rank of Air Commodore.

Four of us were invited to a 21st birthday party by one of the civilian girls who worked on the camp and lived in the Rhondda Valley. Dressed smartly in our uniforms, we caught the late afternoon train from Llantwit Major and after changing trains at Pontypridd arrived at Treorchy late that evening. It was raining and the low black clouds made the night even darker as we walked down the streets between the rows of stone built miner's houses. We had a good time with lots to eat and drink and next morning the girls took us up the mountain (what we had thought the evening before to have been black clouds) to look down into the next valley. Either way the view was almost identical; a small town with tiny houses in long parallel, monotonous terraced streets, roofs slanting against grey hillsides, and within walking distance, the coal mines with their slag heaps. At the pit heads stood the steel lattice work of the winding gear, like metal windmills, their huge wheels spinning, hauling the men to the surface in cages, coal-dust-black and weary from their labours below. In spite of these drab and gloomy surroundings there was a warm and poetic charm about the people, and we were made to feel very welcome in their close-knit community. In the evening we sat in the Pavilion Community Hall to see the film "To Have and Have Not" starring Humphrey Bogart and Lauren Bacall. It would have made our stay perfect if we could have heard the famous Treorchy Male Voice Choir, but it had been disbanded in 1942 owing to war-time difficulties and was not reformed until late 1946, the year we were there. It was to be forty-eight years before I returned to Treorchy with my wife and son, and this dream realised. When they performed at Windsor Castle in the presence of Queen Victoria in 1895, a local journalist wrote that "They behaved like gentlemen and sang like angels".

At that time, in the latter half of the 19th century, the valleys of South Wales filled quickly with mining communities similar to Treorchy, and almost 40, 000 miners had been working in the Rhondda Valley alone. However, demand for coal had begun to decline after 1918 and unemployment rose to almost 50% in the 1930's. The mining industry went into further decline after 1948. The last Pit in Treorchy, the 'Park Coal Mine', closed in 1966 and by the early 1990's, from the 53 pits in the Rhondda that were at one time producing coal, none remained. Since my brief visit in 1946, life must have changed considerably for the people in the Rhondda, once regarded as the most famous mining valley in the world. The landscape had already begun to change as early as the 1960's with afforestation of abandoned land, and in the Rhondda today, in place of the coal mines, some 300 firms of varying sizes produce an extensive range of products.

None of this could be foreseen in 1946 and certainly any change in the people's lifestyle was far from our thoughts as the birthday party continued well into the early hours of the next day. On returning to our huts at the RAF Station in the afternoon, we fell wearily on to our beds in order to catch up with the sleep we had lost the night before.

In our Navy uniforms, I always felt that we looked out of place on an RAF Station. The navy blue 'tops' and bell-bottom trousers, cotton 'white-fronts' (short sleeved shirts) and blue collars with three narrow white tapes stitched round the edge, (reputedly to represent the three Nelson Victories) were a development from the first naval dress of 1857 that had been laid down by the Admiralty. Thankfully, however, we didn't have our hair in pigtails plaited with oakum, which was the custom in the 19th century; neither were earrings allowed, which again were worn about the same time by sailors, in the belief that wearing them would improve their eyesight!

Another part of the uniform we wore dates back even earlier. This was the black silk scarf, or handkerchief, worn round the neck and knotted at the midriff after being folded lengthways to about one-and-a-half inches wide.

This piece of clothing we were told, represented Nelson's funeral. Like the story of the white tapes on the collar, we doubted whether either of these tales was true, but they gave a little 'colour' to the traditional 'Fore-and-Aft' uniform of the Navy. Finally there was the white cord, known as the Lanyard, which we also wore round our neck with our Number 1 uniform, but now had no practical use except for show.

We dressed meticulously and one modern innovation was to put seven creases into the legs of our bell-bottoms. This, supposedly, was to represent the seven seas. It was achieved by turning the trousers inside out and folding each trouser leg separately into seven equal parts. In order to retain the crease, we would run a little soap along each fold before pressing with a hot iron. For everyday use, we wore our Number 2 uniform with the red arm badges, but for 'going ashore' (we always used naval expressions even on shore bases) we put on our Number 1 suit. This was usually made of higher quality serge and purchased by ourselves from the civilian tailor's shop which was on most of the larger shore bases. The arm badges, depicting our trade and rank were made of gold thread. The uniform was made-to-measure and therefore of a much tighter fit than the naval issue and gave us a much neater appearance. To enable us to look like experienced 'sea salts', we wore our hats 'flatter back' (on the back of our heads and against regulations!) when on leave, and bleached our dark collars to a light sky blue. At St. Athan, being an RAF Station, we had no opportunity to purchase a Number 1 uniform but as we wore overalls when at work, we were able to keep our Number 2s fairly smart.

Due to a week I spent in the 'sick-bay' (hospital) with 'flu, I slipped to the class behind the rest of my friends. They naturally finished their training before me and were immediately posted to The Royal Naval Base at Trincomalee in Ceylon. We were to follow. However, the base closed down and they were diverted to another base in Ceylon, and we went to Scotland together with the tropical kit we had been issued with! We didn't meet again until September 1947, just before we were 'de-mobbed'.

After brief spells at HMS 'Siskin' and HMS 'Daedalus', I was posted to HMS 'Sanderling', the Royal Naval Air Station at Abbotsinch near Paisley, Scotland, as a fully-fledged Air Mechanic (Engines). Here I stayed until September 1947 servicing the Rolls Royce Merlin and Griffon engines in the Seafire and Firefly and carrying out the DIs (Daily Inspections) of the aircraft. These inspections included checking fuel levels, filler cap, engine intake, as well as checking that all bolts securing the engine to the airframe were sound, and examining the propeller for wear or peeling of the outer cover. We also ensured that the engines started correctly and the cartridges fired without mishap. These were 'fired' by pressing a button in the cockpit which then turned the starter motor. It was essential for the pilot's safety, of course, that everything worked efficiently. After completion, we would then sign Form 700 and trust that we had done the work to the satisfaction of our Engineering Officer.

Whilst we were stationed at Abbotsinch, we were told that we would be taking part in the Review of the Fleet, and that King George V1 would be 'taking the salute' on the Aircraft Carrier HMS 'Illustrious'. The previous Royal Review had been held off the south coast in 1937 and made famous by a memorable BBC broadcast of the occasion by Lieutenant Commander Woodruff. He was a competent and respected Outside Broadcast Commentator, but on this occasion his friends had been artfully supplying him with drinks. He had left the wardroom of his ship and climbed the masthead to do a commentary on the fleet spread out before him. It didn't go quite as he had intended. . .

"At the present moment the whole fleet's lit up – when I say lit up, I mean lit up – with fairy lamps – we've forgotten the whole Royal Review – we've forgotten the Royal Review – it isn't a fleet at all – it's fairyland – the whole fleet's in fairyland, – this whole huge fleet – lit up – by lights!" At a pre-arranged signal the lights of the fleet were extinguished and he had continued with his hesitant commentary and doing his best to sound sober. . .

"It's gone! – there's no fleet – it's disappeared! – no magician who ever could have waved his wand, could have waved it with more acumen than he has now at the present moment – there's nothing between us and heaven -"

Lord Reith, the Director General of the BBC, had said that he (Woodruff) should have to listen to the record of the broadcast, (no tape recordings in those days) at a board of enquiry and that would be almost punishment enough.

Now 10 years later, we were travelling in buses the 20 miles or so to Gourock through Port Glasgow and Greenock, waving to the crowds lining the route that the Royal Family would be taking later. When on board the aircraft carrier anchored in the centre of the Clyde, I went in search of a school mate of mine who I knew was on the ship. We had a brief chat and didn't meet again until after we were both 'de-mobbed'.

On the flight deck we marched past the King in single file and I, along with all the others, had an uninterrupted view of the Royal Family. It was a great occasion and one that I felt very privileged to take part in. The brief time that I spent on HMS 'Illustrious' was to be my only experience on the sea – unless I include a few trips on the Gosport Ferry across to Portsmouth when I was stationed at HMS 'Daedalus', near Lee-on-Solent!

After a while, some of us became more experienced in the job we were doing and awarded Air Mechanic 1st Class status in February 1947. Not only did this apparently excuse us from doing all night 'Hangar Guard' (they were long, cold and miserable nights on the far side of the airfield) but we were now trusted to do other tasks on the engines, such as the new modifications to the S. U. Carburettor. We appeared also to be better respected by the Officer Engineers and treated more as equals. I always looked forward to going on leave, but in those days the trains often took a long time to get to their destination. On one occasion when returning from leave, the train was hours late getting into Glasgow. It was obvious that I would be 'adrift', (late arriving back without permission) and would be put 'on a charge'. No doubt looking worried at how I was going to get from Glasgow to Paisley and then to RNAS Abbotsinch in about 2 minutes, I was approached by a Sub-Lieutenant and a Wren Officer. They too had been on the same train, and telling me not to worry took me with them and treated me to a breakfast, and then, when we finally arrived at the station, explained to the guard on the gate what had happened and I was waved through. This concern by Naval Officers for only a rating left a great impression on me.

It was the usual practice for an allowance to be made home which was deducted from our pay. This left me with about £2 a fortnight, and after I had sent a £1 at regular intervals to the International Correspondence School for a course I was undertaking, I had little left to spend. Pay day was often celebrated with a few pints of beer in the NAAFI Canteen. I was unable therefore, to go to the cinema in Paisley or Glasgow as often as I would have liked, but the 'Drawing Office and Machine Design' course that I was taking kept me busy when others complained of being bored. I didn't find it easy trying to learn Mathematics, Geometry and Trigonometry from the instruction books, and the exam' papers I submitted were difficult. The 'Practical Drawing' section of the course I also found hard and I only had a small second-hand set of instruments to work with. However, I persevered as I'd set my heart on being a draughtsman when I came out of the Navy.

It was mostly during the week immediately after being paid when we went 'ashore' to Glasgow. The second week found a lot of the lads without money, either because they had spent it quickly or lost it playing 'brag' or 'pontoon'. Often it was because they were left short after paying back what they had borrowed the previous fortnight from the ones who had been more careful. It was my first experience watching the strong exploiting the weak.

I enjoyed writing long letters home and, not having been a reader of books previously, I discovered the enjoyment of a good novel. I particularly liked a popular author at that time, Nevil Shute and read 'Old Captivity', 'Landfall', 'Pied Piper' and 'Most Secret' in quick succession. I found his stories exciting and adventurous and reflecting the eventful time that we had recently lived through. Although Nevil Shute had an Aero-Nautical career as well as being a novelist, he was commissioned in the Royal Navy Volunteer

Reserve in 1940, rose to lieutenant-Commander in 1941 and retired from the RNVR in 1945.

Another thing I discovered whilst in the Navy, was a love of Grand Opera. We had at home a few HMV Red Label 12" records of popular classical music which I enjoyed and I had been to a concert with my brother at Coventry Hippodrome during the war, but I'd never been to an opera. My only experience was listening to a recording of 'Madam Butterfly' on the wireless with Dad. We sat in the dark to enable us to concentrate and I thought Puccini's music was wonderful. I must have been 15 or 16 years old at the time. Now, a group of us were going to the opera at the Theatre Royal in Glasgow to see Wagner's 'The Flying Dutchman'. The others had been when the Carl Rosa Opera Company had visited the theatre on a previous occasion, and they knew their opera. I had a mental picture of sitting in an expensive seat which I couldn't really afford, among all the gentry of Glasgow, as a soprano of enormous proportions stood at the front of the stage in a spotlight, giving full voice to the resounding music of Wagner. I had no idea what I was in for and my friends wouldn't tell me. "Wait and see", they said.

It turned out to be nothing like I had imagined. My first surprise was when we went past the brightly lit front of the theatre and joined a small queue in a dark side street about three-quarters of an hour before the performance was due to begin. At a tiny box office just inside the door, we paid two shillings each (ten pence), and climbed a narrow stone staircase to 'heaven'. Eventually we found ourselves in the only area of the theatre where standing was permitted – behind the back row of the 'gods'. We looked down at a fairly steep angle to the small stage below. I was completely disillusioned until the lights went out, the Overture began and the curtain rose on a truly magical setting. I was enthralled and I became completely absorbed in the music and singing of the performance of the 1st Act of this Wagnerian Opera. During the interval, an usherette found a seat for me, and I sat next to an ex-sailor who told me that he'd booked seats for three more operas for himself and a friend who had not been able to come after all but had not returned his tickets. If I paid my 2/- each time, he suggested, I could have his friend's seat if I was interested in coming. I managed to get away to see all three and loved them all. It was the beginning of my life-long love of Grand Opera.

The Carl Rosa Company's policy of presenting opera in English provided invaluable training ground to many singers and at that time had artists who included Gwen Catley, Victoria Elliot, Joan Hammond, Norman Allin, Tudor Davies, Arthur Tear, Heddle Nash, Otakar Kraus and Parry Jones. Their main conductors were Peter Gellhorn, Arthur Hammond, Walter Susskind and Vilem Tausky. The Company was founded in 1875 by Karl August Nicholas Rose, or Carl Rosa as he became later. He was a German violinist and conductor and formed the company to present opera in English. They opened at the The Gaiety Theatre in Dublin on 29 March 1875. Its first London Season began on 11 September of that year at the Princess's Theatre with 'Le nozze di Figaro'. In 1877 they performed at the Theatre Royal in Glasgow and visited regularly thereafter. In 1897 the Company put on the first performance in this country of the now popular, Puccini's 'La Boheme'.

Running into financial difficulties in 1948 (the year after I first saw them) the company eventually received a Grant from the Arts Council totalling £61, 000 in the five years after 1953, but at the end of 1958, Sadlers Wells took over some of the company's personnel and the short lived 'Touring Company 1958' was formed. Their existence came to an end with a performance of 'Don Giovanni' on 17 September 1960. After I came out of the Navy, I saw them on a number of occasions in theatres in Coventry, Leicester and Stratford-on-Avon.

Prior to leaving Abbotsinch to return to HMS 'Daedalus' from where I would be 'de-mobbed', we were given an opportunity to take a two weeks EVTC (Education and Vocational Training Course) at Stafford. The course was mainly designed for those who had been in the RAF or RNAS for some time, and to help to prepare them to return to 'civvi-street', but it was available for all. Few took advantage of it. I wanted to spend most of my time there catching up with my correspondence course, and in particular, making use of the drawing boards and equipment at the Centre. There were also lectures on a variety of subjects and I took the opportunity to go to one or two of them, especially enjoying the one on poetry. I found the poems of contemporary poets like Louis McNeice, Dylan Thomas, C. Day Lewis, John Betjeman and particularly Robert Frost fresh and exciting. They were in complete contrast to the ones we had learnt at school by Yeats, Browning, Wordsworth and 1st World War poets like Rupert Brook. Henry Reed's 'Naming of Parts' fascinated me and the contrasts in the poem were beautifully expressed. I also found it amusing as I recalled the way that I, too, had learned about the rifle from my instructor.

At HMS 'Daedalus', I chose a raincoat, a blue herring-bone pattern 'de-mob' suit, blue trilby hat, two shirts, a tie and some socks, and set off for home, excited at the prospect that I would soon be working in a drawing office. I wrote letters to factories in Coventry and had interviews but the answer was always the same : I had no experience of the work for my age and I would soon have to be paid a man's wage while I was still learning the job.

I sat with my brother in his house, completely disillusioned and disappointed, and wondering whether I would have to return to my office job at the quarry after all. The insurance man called to collect the premiums. He was a Mr Dingley, of the Pearl Assurance.

"Looking for a job?" he said to me.

"Yes", I replied, "and without success".

He puffed at his pipe, "You can have this one if you want it".

His pipe had gone out and he struck a match and re-lit it.

"I'm the Assistant District Manager and I'm looking for a new agent to fill this book", he continued, "so perhaps you'd like to come for an interview".

# CHAPTER SEVEN

# LONG STREET

I commenced work as a Pearl Assurance Collector (later to be re-designated as District Agent)on Friday 12th December 1947, a month before my twentieth birthday. The Assistant District Manager, Mr. Dingley, who had offered me the job introduced me to the 'debit', and for the next two weeks we called on most of the houses and policyholders I was to visit for the next seventeen years in the town and surrounding villages of Warwickshire and Leicestershire.

Atherstone had changed very little from the 1930s and shops and businesses had hardly altered, from Rogerson's Garage on the corner of Station Street at the 'bottom end' of Long Street, to the Regal Cinema at the 'top' which had opened in 1937 and had been built on the site of the old workhouse. Opposite Rogerson's Garage there was the bay-windowed house of Mr. Rumsey, our dentist, and a few yards further on, the premises of Percy Vero, the Funeral Director. For a short time, I rented one of his garages for my first small car, and he would tell me how as a young man, he would take the Prudential Agent and his Inspector around to the farms in the district, canvassing for business. It was a journey which used to take him all day in his pony and trap.

I called on a number of the very old houses that still remained in the 'yards'. Before the war, some of these 'yards' had been pulled down and the people re-housed in Council Houses, but quite a lot of the houses still remained and were in poor condition with no inside plumbing or toilets, and wash-houses shared by a number of residents.

Opposite Eastaff's sweet shop (I went to school with their son Kenneth)was the office and yard of Frank Miles, coal merchants. The office, with its large window, was very bare with a huge solid wooden counter separating the public from the other side where Miss Doris Miles did the office work. She was very tall and held her head down at a slight angle, rounding her shoulders as if conscious of her height. Her dark hair, cut short, was beginning to turn grey when I first called and she always greeted me with a smile and "How is Mr. John today?". Then sometimes she would invite me to take a sugary sweet from a box she kept hidden from her brother Frank. Next door was Gisbourne's tobacconist, and (a few doors further on) C. B. Collins' grocery shop where I had worked as a delivery boy and shop assistant. Just beyond Woolworth's on the opposite side of the road, I was always given an early Saturday morning cup of tea at a house I called on behind Stan Green's newsagent shop. He was the same Stan Green who played at the Town Hall dances on Saturday nights. I called on Mrs. Vero at the delicatessen, where I occasionally treated myself to a jar of Rose's Lime Marmalade, and then further along to a Mr. Webber, our family hairdresser. On one occasion when I called at the shop, I met a man I had known in the Navy who was now a commercial traveller dealing in toiletries. During training we had both been the tallest in the class, and therefore natural opponents for one of the compulsory boxing matches we had to participate in. I noticed that he was still about four stone heavier than me, and during the match when he had hit me twice with what felt like a sledgehammer, the physical training instructor had stopped the contest. I believe the phrase was, "to stop me from receiving further punishment."

Opposite Webber's was the Co-operative Grocery store and also the Men's Department where I bought my first suit when I had come out of the Navy. I had had to use my clothing coupons of course, as clothes rationing didn't end until March 1949. Stringer's Greengrocery and Fishmonger's shop was a few doors further on, where pheasants and rabbits often hung up outside. Many of the shops had been, and still were, family businesses, including the two shops owned by the Pickering family. One was a Jewellers and Opticians, and next door the Music Shop where I bought all my records – Ray Pickering, the Scoutmaster, was a nephew of the owners and when his aunt and uncle retired he ran the shop until he too retired.

Between Church Street and Market Street was one of the two Chemists in the town, Parkinson's. When we did our first Scout Show in 1964, Doreen Parkinson, who was involved with the Atherstone Amateur Dramatic Society, organised the make-up team for the show. Opposite was Masters' Bakery and Confectionery Shop. Two of the brothers who owned the shop were also, for a while, Directors of Atherstone Town Football Club. For two years between 1956 and 1958, I edited the official programme for the club and many a time I had to wait in the bakehouse watching them make bread and cakes, as they discussed and decided on the team for the following Saturday before I could take it, together with my 'jottings', to the printers in Market Street. The 'Adders' never again reached the heights of the 1947-48 season when they won the Birmingham Senior Cup and were League Winners of the Birmingham Combination.

Hiscock's shop extended from Long Street through to Market Street and had many departments including carpets and furniture. On the corner was the 'Men's Shop', run for many years by Walter Whiteman. His father was a well-known South Junior School teacher who rapped many an inattentive pupil's head with the ring on his middle finger – and very painful it was too! The main departments were Drapery and Haberdashery, and they all had a 'payment for goods' system which was common to many other large Department Stores of the 1930's and 40's. Cash and the bill were put into a metal container which was then transported through tubes to the office pay desk by air pressure. The receipt and change were returned to the shop assistant by the same method.

Next door to Hiscock's was a Newsagents and Stationery Shop, which was also the office for the weekly 'Atherstone News' paper. The proprietor of the shop, Mrs. Coleman, was also the editor and we always looked forward to reading the 'News' every Friday. A couple of doors further on was Cleelands' Shoe Shop, managed by a Mr. Devy. It was he and George Kimber, a quarryman, who were the morse instructors for the Air Training Corps. It was Mr. Devy who broke the news to me on that ill-fated day in the beginning of February 1958, that the 'plane carrying the brilliantly talented Manchester United football team had crashed in Munich and that most of the team were dead. Only two months earlier I had seen them play Birmingham City at St. Andrews, in an exciting 3-3 draw. The team had been built up by their Manager, Mat Busby, and they were so much more than a football team. Television had brought their young players into the homes of people who wouldn't normally have watched a football match, and now it was hard to believe that we wouldn't see the 'Busby Babes' play again. Between Bindley's greengrocery shop and the corner of Coleshill Road was the Co-op Butcher's. Mr. Evans was the manager there for many years and his house in Stanley Road, was one of my last calls on Saturday afternoon. On Cup Final Day in 1953, his wife Olive, invited me to watch the match on their new 7" screen television set. Not everyone had this new invention in their homes at that time. It was the famous 'Stanley Matthews Match' in which every football supporter was hoping that he would at last get a Cup Final

Winner's Medal. His team, Blackpool, were 1-3 down with only half-an-hour to go before the final whistle. Then amid great excitement, and inspired by his skilful play, they won the match 4-3! It was a memorable game and a thrill to watch the Cup Final instead of listening to the commentary on the wireless as we had done previously.

Other well-known and established family businesses included Tom Adcock's baker's shop – who supplied the meat pies which were sold to the quarrymen for 4d – and Jenkins' baker's and confectioner's where my sister was shop assistant for a while after leaving school. There was Harry Spittle's Shoe Shop, where you could get every type of footwear from slippers to pit-boots: I used to buy my shoes from there by just quoting the number stamped inside the shoe. Nearby was Lock's, one of the two ironmongers of the town. If you waited to ask Laurence, the shop assistant, if they had what you were looking for, and described it to him in great detail: "a screw at one end with a piece sticking up in the middle, and a long tapering thing for going into a whatsit", – he'd find it for you in one of the many boxes behind the counter.

Further down the road, Mr. Garratt was a boot and shoe repairer. His three sons had all been members of the scouts. He would hop around the shop on his one leg, and stoke up his coke-fired stove which heated the large wooden hut he worked in. There was Grubb's newsagent's (opposite Denham and Hargraves Hat Factory), Fox's butcher's in the 'hollow', and Shilton's greengrocery on the corner of Welcome Street. This street was reputedly named as such when Florence Nightingale had come to Atherstone to stay with the Bracebridge family at Atherstone Hall. In Welcome Street was the Parish Room where we were later to 'stage' a very amateurish Scout Show production. Almost opposite in Long Street, next to 'The Dolphin' pub, was the site where the Scouts were eventually to build their own first Headquarters.

In the centre of the town were the Council Offices. Before going into the Navy I had belonged to the 'Junior Council', which met in the Council Chamber of the building. We would air our views on the topics that were being discussed by the main Rural District Council. I don't think that we were taken seriously, however, and the Junior Council had had a very short life. Nearby was Farmer's Cycle Shop where I bought my first motorised transport – a 'New Hudson' Auto-cycle. Between Farmer's and the Council Offices was the General Post Office. Being a keen stamp collector, I paid regular visits in order to keep up-to-date with the new issues. My brother Ron paid even more regular visits when he fell in love with one of the counter clerks, Kathleen, the Post Master's daughter, and married her.

I have only mentioned some of the shops and businesses but there were many others in the town, of course, and almost all of them had been there since before the war. Frank Adcock, brother of Tom, had his own cake shop further down the town next to Barnsley's Wool Shop where you could also buy a jar of Mr. Barnsley's own honey. There were a number of small sweet shops which also sold groceries, including Hunt's, Barsby's, Gale's in Market Street and Wood's at the bottom of 'Polly Cook's' yard. There was also the 'Candy Stores' which sold only sweets and ice-cream. Two other bakers were Green's and Beeby's, and butchers included Bates in Market Street and the two shops owned by Reg' Tunbridge, one of which had a slaughter-house at the back, supplying both shops. There were a couple more shoe repairers in the town, and another two tobacconists, Hick's, and Chetwynd's in Church Street. Men's Hairdressers were Bill Bayliss in Market Street and Webster's in 'The Hollow' (Long Street), opposite Wainwright's Garage – the Rover Car dealer.

The other chemist was Ison's, with huge richly coloured glass jars in the window, and containers on shelves behind the counter engraved with the names of every ingredient used in medicines. Megginson's was the other ironmongers, and Brown's Furniture Shop was where my parents had bought most of their furniture when they came to Atherstone in 1925. As well as the small shops there were the usual multiple grocers of Pearks, Melias, The Star, The Maypole, and another shop similar to Collins, Goodwin Foster Brown's – known colloquially as GFB's.

Lloyds and Midland were the only two Banks, apart from the Co-op, and there were some twenty public houses and Clubs within the shopping area of the town, so no-one went thirsty! Finally there was the indomitable police force led by Inspector Bailey, supported by Sergeant Pearson, and Sergeant Wilmot (later Inspector Wilmot) and, among others, the well respected and sometimes feared, PC Painting. He was a real friendly 'copper', but his impending appearance on his cycle was sufficient to prevent the petty offender from carrying out his intentions, and quickly become an apparently innocent bystander. However, he was a 'stickler' for the law and woe betide anyone he caught breaking it!

Miss Ivy Mulford, secretary for many years to the Town Clerk, Mr May, invited me to be a Poll Clerk at a Polling Station at the 1950 General Election. After that I continued to help at subsequent Local and General Elections, eventually aspiring to the role of Presiding Officer. I was well paid, and I found it interesting as I knew so many people. It also gave me the appearance of not being in sympathy with any particular political party, which suited me very nicely in my job with the Pearl.

I was told that working as an agent for an Assurance Company was generally regarded to be a trustworthy and privileged position. It was also pointed out to me that there were only three types of people who could knock at a door and immediately walk in, without waiting to be invited, the doctor, the clergy, and the insurance man. There were very few houses where I couldn't do this, and often the money and premium receipt books were left for me, either on the sideboard or kitchen table. Sometimes I might have to let myself in with the key which had been left in an outhouse. I think it extremely doubtful if anything like this happens today!

Our earnings were a combination of salary and commissions which we deducted each week from our collections. However, if we failed to balance our accounts – and there were many ways how this could happen – we couldn't get away with telling our District Manager that our wages were correct but the Pearl was a few pounds short! In my first year I earned £322 and paid £23 in income tax. After four years my earnings had increased to £465, and in the March of that year 1951, I married. The first time that I earned over £1000 a year (a 'target' wage at the time)was not until 1964, the same year that I was promoted to Assistant District Manager at Burton-on-Trent. During the seventeen years as an agent, I had called on houses in almost every street of the town and in numerous villages within a four mile radius of Atherstone.

In the early years I didn't find completing new business very easy, especially in the Ordinary Branch. New business was generally confined to the Industrial Branch and collected weekly. Children's endowments were limited to a weekly premium of one shilling and sixpence – providing there wasn't already a penny life policy in force – then the maximum was one shilling and a penny.

During our working week, if we completed new business totalling 5/- or more in weekly premiums, we were in the 'Honours List' on the notice board. I once completed 15 proposals for £1 and came top of the G (Birmingham) Division.

There was little or no House Purchase business done at this time and the Company were many years away from writing Unit Funds. The emphasis was on Endowments and Whole Life with the General Branch confined mainly to writing Domestic Fire Insurance, and insurance on motor cycles and cars. Most people paid premiums for Household Fire Insurance of 4/- (four shillings) per year for £200 of contents cover, and when the Company increased the minimum premium to 6/-, with a corresponding rise in the sum insured, some people refused to pay. One could insure a 350cc motor cycle for less than £4 a year for Comprehensive cover excluding damage to the vehicle. A small car would be about £10 with 20% maximum no claim discount. The annual Road Tax was £10 and as late as 1953, a Ford Popular was only £390 to buy new, – but very few people had cars in 1947.

When I started with the Pearl, apart from the District Manager and the Assistant District Manager, only one other member of the staff had a car, and for the first nine years a pedal cycle was my only transport. Then, following the auto-cycle which I bought in 1956, I purchased a second-hand three wheeler Bond Mini-Car for £330. It had a 198cc Villiers engine mounted over the front wheel but apart from a number of frightening and sometimes humorous incidents, it proved to be very reliable. I kept it for about three years before changing to a Morris Mini-Van and two years later when I was promoted I bought a Ford Anglia – my first real car.

# CHAPTER EIGHT

# NEW AGE

On Saturday evenings many of us went out of town to the dance at Dordon Village Hall. It was about three miles from Atherstone and usually meant a walk back afterwards getting home about midnight. It was a welcome change from the Town Hall, which in any case, was soon to be condemned as being structurally unsafe. I had been many times even before going into the Navy, and again when I came home on leave. It was always a good dance with a first class band and everyone seemed to have a good time. The M.C.,Archie Rooms, would come to the microphone and with a broad smile announce in his soft spoken voice:

"And the next dance – is a quick-step."

As soon as the Ivor Pope band began to play, we would move quickly to the girls of our choice in order to be first on the floor, and have plenty of room to do the 'reverse turns' or a 'double lock' without being jostled by others. Soon the floor would be full of couples, some doing just the basic steps and some 'jitterbugging'. During the evening, Archie would announce Ladies Invitation Dances, 'Excuse me' quick-steps, waltzes, slow fox-trots, tangos and, for a bit of fun and light relief, 'old fashioned'dances, such as The

Valeta, Military Two-Step or the Gay Gordons.

There was a good friendly atmosphere at these dances and we enjoyed ourselves and made many new friends. Four of us became quite close and together went to Llandudno in North Wales, for our summer holiday in 1948. During the week we took a boat trip to the Isle of Man, and I did more sailing on that day than I had done in the two years I spent in the Royal Navy!

In the previous March, the four of us had been invited to Sheila Sutton's 21st Birthday Dance at Sheepy Village Hall. It was the same day as the Grand National, and as Sheila lived in the first bungalow as one entered the village, we all naturally had a bet on a horse called Sheila's Cottage in the race, to come in the first three. As the bookies had only given it odds of 33 to 1, no one had any illusions of it winning – but it did! It made the evening much more enjoyable, especially as I normally would never bet on horses. I won about two pounds five shillings, – equivalent to over a third of my week's wages – for a stake of 1/- each way. However, it caused me a few problems. During my Saturday morning's round, I had told people the story of why I was 'backing' this horse and quite a number of people had won money. They therefore now regarded me as a lucky 'tipster', and for a number of weeks after that, as soon as I entered their house, they would greet me with, "What's going to win the 2.30?"

Four years later three of us had married and together with our wives went on holiday to Ilfracombe. We didn't have cars, so we journeyed by rail changing at Barnstaple to the local train which took us to the holiday resort. After travelling through Braunton and Morthoe, the last part of the journey gave us a magnificent panoramic view of the coast, and from the high positioned railway station, we looked down to the picturesque town of Ilfracombe sited between the cliffs and hills of the surrounding countryside. We were content for a few minutes just to look at the view until a taxi took us to our Guest House overlooking the small harbour with the

Coronation Bonfire Guard 1937

Berkswell Camp 1939

Dad – Blackpool 1930

With Ron and Audrey 1931

With Dad's Mother and Mum 1932

134 Coleshill Road

The Beehive

Grandpa 1951

Mum's Parents

Toll Gate House

St. Mary's Church and Town Hall

Long Street

Shrove Tuesday

Merevale Hall

Mum and Dad 1946

Aged 19

Scout Show 1967

Easter Camp1962

"The Coldest Night-"

'The Twentyone Oaks'

RSPB Stall Grimsby 1991

fishing boats moored alongside the quay. We hired that same driver during the week, to take us to the best places to visit in that part of North Devon which, of course, was all new to us. He was a colourful character with a rich Devonshire accent, and gave us an account of the places we visited embellishing them with anecdotes and folklore. Some of the stories we believed and some we didn't, or at least doubted their authenticity.

On the first day that he took us out, he pointed along the coast towards Lynton.

"Those two hills over there," he said, "are known as 'Hangman's Hills'. In the last century, if you stole a sheep they'd hang you from the 'Great Hangman's', and if you stole a lamb, you'd be hanged from the the 'Little Hangman's'- that's the origin of the saying, 'you might as well be hung for a sheep as a lamb'.." We listened to many stories like that one, wondering whether they were true. He was a good storyteller. He took us to many interesting places including the 11th Century St.Petrock's Church at Parracombe, the Valley of Rocks at Lynton and the beautiful scenic harbour at Lynmouth.

Here, fuchsias and hydrangeas in full bloom flanked the sides of the two streams, the East and West Lyn, which joined together in the village and ran into the miniature harbour. A cliff railway, nine hundred feet long with a gradient of one in one-and-three-quarters, links Lynmouth with Lynton 500 feet above and for the passengers affords excellent views over the area. The lovely old cottages, the thatched 'Rising Sun' Inn at the foot of Mars Hill, and the trees covering the steep slopes and valleys, created a picture of peace and tranquillity. The little Rhenish Tower on the harbour wall and the fishing and sailing boats in the harbour, gave the whole scene an air of enchantment. Two weeks later on the 15th August, Lynmouth suffered an enormous flood disaster which destroyed the village and killed 34 people.

The rainfall at the beginning of the month in North Devon had been high, soaking the heather on the high moorland areas. Before it had chance to drain away, over nine inches of rain fell on Friday, August 12 following a cloudburst. There was nowhere for it to go and within hours streams had turned into raging torrents, carrying trees and boulders which smashed into the bridges, destroying them. Everything was swept down the East and West Lyn rivers at an alarming speed and the water rose rapidly. Lynmouth was hit by thousands of tons of water, rubble and huge boulders, which quickly destroyed almost a hundred buildings.

Remarkably, work was carried out very quickly to try and restore the village to its former glory, and although the rivers were widened and modern bridges built, it still remains one of the prettiest places in this part of Devon. I have been since on many occasions and at different times of the year, and during one of our visits (in 1980) this resort on the North Devon coast had a little more to offer than I had anticipated. We were staying with our friends from Scouting days in Atherstone, Ron and June Young who now had a Guest House in Lynton. Ron invited me to go with him to Ilfracombe in his boat, a Westerley 'Nomad' with the intriguing name of 'Sam Scratch'. I am no sailor, and as previously explained my only sea-faring experience whilst in the Navy had been limited to one short trip on the Clyde and a few more across Gosport Ferry!

It wasn't a particularly pleasant morning, with an overcast sky and low cloud base but June had given us a hearty breakfast of bacon, eggs, sausage, toast and marmalade, and I was determined that I was going to enjoy myself. All went well as we left the harbour, the boat rolling gently in the slight swell as we headed out into the Bristol Channel. We were going in the direction of Tenby, in South Wales, and even with my limited experience, I was aware that we would soon need to 'turn left' in order to reach our destination.

When we did turn to port (I was beginning to remember the nautical terms I'd learnt in the Navy) everything happened. The boat suddenly began to 'pitch', and the horizon rose and fell as if the world was being moved by some cosmic force. My breakfast quickly left my stomach and I felt that I was going to die. Ron saw my distress, and in the theory that if I had something to do I'd forget about my discomfort, handed me the tiller. He then gave me a 'crash course' – lasting about two minutes – on how to steer a 22 foot sailing cruiser off the rocky coast of North Devon.

I was still being very sea-sick as the boat tossed about like a cork on the now much more choppy sea, and then it began to rain. Without taking my hand off the tiller, I struggled into some oilskins that Ron had thrown up to me from inside the cabin, and then from his cramped position, proceeded to tell me how to work the radio.

"You'll need to know about this", he said, (well, shouted really) so that I could hear him above the noise of the wind, which was not only flapping the sails above me, but unmercifully driving the rain into my face and threatening to dislodge the oilskin hood off my head.

"You'll need to know about this", he repeated, "and how to alert the coast guards if I get swept over-board".

If only he could have read my thoughts, as I clung a little tighter to the tiller, he would have known that I was thinking that 'if he gets swept over-board, I'm going with him'.

We had now been motor sailing for about 2 hours and as we had the ebb-tide, we were now doing about 6 knots. The rain stopped as quickly as it had started, the wind dropped and the sun came out as we entered the harbour at Ilfracombe. Ron 'messed about' with the sails, and I began to feel good as holiday-makers looked enviously at the two sailors who had just brought in their little boat from 'heaven knows where'. We were also very hungry – me especially – and we enjoyed the bacon sandwiches that June had thoughtfully packed for us.

We had the Spring-tide with us on the way back, and being clear of a very choppy sea off Baggy Point, Ron unfurled both the Genoa

Sail and the Main Sail – sailing Goosewinged. However, the calmer waters did not prevent the fishes from having another feed, this time of my partly digested lunch. As we approached Lynmouth harbour, dropping the sails and motoring in, I saw some of the old local boatmen watching us come past the Rhenish Tower. We appeared to be almost the last ones in, and as Ron steered the boat towards our moorings, he gave me a grappling pole (as I believe it was called) to hook round a rope in order to slow down our progress. Even at full stretch there was no way I could reach that rope, and we hit the harbour wall with a little too much force. The old-salts' faces watching us from over the wall were expressionless. I tried not to read their thoughts.

Clambering aboard a dinghy, we made our way across the harbour between the boats, watched all the way from above. Nearing the iron ladder – vertical against the wall – my 'skipper' told me to hold on to a rope nearby to stop us from drifting past. I did as I was instructed, not wishing to embarrass my friend further in front of the 'locals', but unfortunately pulled a little too hard. We went shooting by, and only Ron's quick presence of mind to hang on to something prevented us from circumnavigating the harbour. I looked up at those weather-beaten faces. They puffed on their pipes and spat into the water. They'd seen it all before.

The following morning, my discomfiture on the previous day's trip forgotten, the adventure had added a new dimension to my fondness for that beautiful part of North Devon. Now I was content to walk through the woods alongside the East Lyn to Watersmeet, and stroll in the evening on the North Walk around Hollerday Hill to the Valley of Rocks, as the white light from the sun – low in the sky – created dancing lights in the sea, three or four hundred feet below. If Lynmouth had changed a little after the carnage and destruction of 1952, the coastal scenery was as lovely as ever.

When we had been there at the end of July in that year, there had been no sign of any impending disaster about to hit this North

Devon resort, and as the weather was fine and warm at the week-end we were due to return home, four of us stayed on for an extra two days to enable us to visit Lundy Island. As it was now Sunday we wore our best clothes, which was hardly the ideal attire for sailing on the ferry boat,or scrambling about in dinghies as we were carried ashore to the island's small landing stage. I wanted to go across the island to look at the sea birds, but our time was very short and we were soon joining the long queue waiting our turn to be taken back to the ship.

We returned home, spending our last few shillings on a more expensive rail ticket, which entitled us to sit in the observation coach of the train enjoying the view. These coaches had a large expanse of window and were positioned at the end of the train.

During the early post-war years, food rationing, in regard to some items, was almost as bad as during the war. The weekly ration was reduced to two-and-a-half pints of milk and one-and-a-half ounces of cheese per person in June 1947. The milk ration went down even further to only two pints in 1948.

Also at this time, the Government embarked on radical changes in the way the country was run and particularly in regard to the ownership of large industrial concerns. The labour Government, which had been elected in 1945, nationalised the Coal Mines on January 1st 1947, the British Railways on January 1st 1948, and the British Electrical Industry on April 1st in the same year.

The large Assurance Companies saw the Nationalisation policy as a real threat to their industry, and indeed, it was strongly advocated to be next in line for public ownership. This was the reason for the Industrial Life Offices Association to be formed. Money was found by the companies to enable branches to be set up in every large town. Insurance men from the life assurance companies were automatically members, and formed committees to arrange meetings and organise an Annual Luncheon. The sole purpose of this luncheon, to which local dignatories and representatives from all walks of life were invited, was to publicise the achievements of the Assurance Companies, and to stress the importance of them remaining free to invest their funds into industry, for the benefit of the country as a whole. The companies were also concerned that, if their huge premium income and reserves were controlled by public ownership, not only would dividends to shareholders disappear, but bonuses would be drastically reduced. Furthermore, there was a real fear among the companies' employees that there would be a big reduction in staff, as often two or three insurance men called in the same house.

The ILO, as it was known, was well supported by all the large Industrial Life Offices except one, which had political allegiance with the party in government. In October 1951 there was a change in Government as the Conservatives were returned with a small majority, and the threat seen by the companies to their industry went away.

During that period, however, some insurance men found they had a conflict of loyalties. Most company employees belonged to a trade union and we were members at that time of the NAULAW (National Amalgamated Union of Life Assurance Workers) affiliated to the TUC, which of course, was closely associated with the Labour Party, and the Government of the day. Some said that we couldn't be loyal to both organisations; we should be either strong trade unionists or loyal ILO supporters! We resolved the problem by joining our 'shop union' NUPA (National Union of Pearl Agents) which had no political affiliations and dealt only with Pearl matters.

In addition to our regular Regional Meetings, we attended the annual West Midlands Area Council Meetings and met and talked with colleagues from other Company Divisions. These were held in turn at Worcester, Wolverhampton and Birmingham. As well as discussing our working practices (and always our inadequate remunerations!) it became a social occasion and an event we looked forward to.

Each year too, we had a staff outing from the office in Nuneaton, spending the day at Henley Regatta or Windsor, visiting the Cotswolds or perhaps a longer trip to Skegness or Blackpool. In 1951 we went to the Festival of Britain in London, on the South Bank of the Thames. This was an event promoting Britain, and included temporary structures built specially for the occasion: – the Dome of Discovery housing exhibits and standing like a huge mushroom in contrast to the tall slim Skylon, and the permanent and very modern Festival Hall.

The Festival had been opened by the King from the steps of St.Paul's in May and nine months later, after a long illness, he died at Sandringham aged only 56. A lot had happened in our lives since that lighting of the bonfire in the Outwoods on the day of his Coronation, and at the beginning of the war, he had spoken to the nation in his Christmas broadcast of 1939 as Britain faced the dark days ahead, and brought comfort and hope to many people, quoting lines from 'The Desert' by M.Louise Haskins:- "And I said to the man who stood at the gate of the year – 'Give me a light that I may tread safely into the unknown'. And he replied, 'Go out into the darkness and put your hand into the hand of God. That shall be to you better than a light and safer than a known way'-"

All that was in the past and we looked forward to what some were saying was going to be a new Elizabethan Age. It started well in the year of the Queen's Coronation with the announcement that Everest had been climbed for the first time by a British team led by Colonel Hunt. Gordon Richards won his first Derby and Stanley Matthews a Cup Final Winner's Medal with his team of Blackpool. England regained the 'Ashes' and there were successes too for British athletes, breaking world records in the marathon (Jim Peters), the six miles (Gordon Pirie) and the mile relay, (the team including Christopher Chataway and Roger Bannister).

My earnings were now over £9 per week, (almost £2 above the

national average) but I was still unable to afford a new house which cost about £2,000 for a three bedroom semi-detached. Most things were now back in the shops and in the following year, 1954, all food rationing ended.

My two daughters were born in the 1950's, Lynn in 1953, and Kay four years later in 1957. Between these dates I bought a small house in Innage Terrace near to the centre of Atherstone for £450, and with the aid of a Council grant and a small overdraft from my bank, I was able to do the repairs necessary to improve the property and convert a bedroom into a bathroom.

The years between the end of the war and this 'new age' had been ones of world tension between East and West, and the full extent of the 'Cold War' culminated in the Soviet Blockade of Berlin in 1948. Now in the middle '50's, the 'Iron Curtain' lifted a little as two football teams came from the Eastern Bloc to play in England. Both Spartak from the USSR and Honved from Hungary sent teams to play one of the leading English Clubs of the day, Wolverhampton Wanderers. I went with the Manager of the Co-op., Mr Webster (father of Gordon who later became Venture Scout Leader) to Molineux to watch both matches. They were played in fog, and even with the floodlights it was impossible to see what was happening at the other end of the pitch. Most of the goals were scored at the opposite end to where we were standing, and we had to rely on the spectators cheering to know when this happened, but there was a great crowd friendliness and an unforgettable atmosphere. There seemed to be no limit to the amount of spectators allowed in to see these matches, and it took a long time to get into the grounds. On one occasion we had only reached the steps to the area behind the goal when we heard the National Anthems being played. Some 'joker' shouted "take yer hats off", but we were packed so tight we couldn't even move our arms and I do believe that my feet weren't even on the floor! At half-time it took us most of the interval to manoeuvre our flask of coffee to a position to enable us to pour the contents into our cups.

I only ever played in one match myself, and this was when I was invited to play in a team with some lads that I had met at Tech in 1944. They were short of a player for their match the following Saturday, and as I was tall they thought I would be suitable to play full-back position. I bought a new pair of football boots from Cleelands (Mr Devy) and turned up at Nuneaton Football Ground to play for Arley Rectory, looking every bit like the player my friends expected me to be. I missed the ball more often than I kicked it; the team lost five goals to nil and they never asked me to play again!

My cricket career lasted even shorter than that. Again making up a team – this time for Atherstone that was one man short – and believing that I could make a name for myself, I didn't see the first three balls that were sent down and the fourth one knocked my stumps out of the ground.

"That wasn't a very good stroke", I said, trying to excuse my inexperience as I walked off the pitch.

"You never made one!" an unkindly spectator answered.

Jack Ball, who played regularly for Atherstone, and could hit a fast fifty runs when in the mood, suffered the same fate as me a few balls later, but not for the same reason. He was at least attempting to hit the ball over mid-on's head, and possibly the boundary for six! However, it made me feel a little bit better that one or 'our' best players followed me into the pavilion after receiving only two more balls than I had before getting dismissed. They, too, never asked me to play again!

I enjoyed watching County Cricket and took every opportunity to go to Edgbaston to see the Warwickshire team play. I also looked forward to their matches at Courtaulds in Coventry every year and their usual fixture with Leicestershire at Hinckley, about seven miles from Atherstone. They were a good entertaining side led by Tom Dollery when I first went to see them, and under his captaincy were County Champions in 1951. The first Test Match I went to was also at Edgbaston when England played the West Indies in 1957. It was a memorable match with Peter May and Colin Cowdrey having a record partnership for the fourth wicket of 411. The year before, Jim Laker of Surrey had taken all ten Australian wickets of their first innings in the Test at Manchester (in fact he took nineteen in the match!) and when he came on to bowl against the West Indies side, their supporters became quite agitated. They jumped up and down in the seats shouting,

"Ten-man Laker, ten-man Laker" to the amusement of the crowds.

I went to the next test at Nottingham and remember Peter May driving the ball hard trying to penetrate the off-side field often without success, due to the brilliant West Indian fielding but eventually reaching his century. Tom Graveney by contrast, scored all around the wicket displaying every one of his masterly strokes, scoring 258 and 164. England had some very good batsmen in these Tests, but Tom Graveney's innings in my view, put him in a league above most of his contempories. I believe he was the most complete batsman I ever saw.

Atherstone was well situated for both these venues where Test Cricket was played, as well as being a reasonable distance from good football grounds where I was able to see First Division games. Villa Park, home of Aston Villa, was one of the quickest to get to, closely followed by St. Andrew's where Birmingham City played. The Hawthorns, home of West Bromwich Albion was not much further, and Filbert Street, Leicester City's ground, was also not too long a journey.

When I moved to Burton-on-Trent in 1964, I missed the Saturday afternoon outings and being now in Staffordshire few people seemed interested in County Cricket, although Trent Bridge was now a little nearer than it had been for me previously. I did, however, still go to Edgbaston whenever I could, as well as Nottingham to see Test Matches, before I moved to Boston in 1977.

Although I was now much further away from the Birmingham Football grounds, the Baseball Ground at Derby was less than ten miles from my new home. Soon after I moved, I went to see them play Manchester United, but it was a frightening experience. There was a new generation of 'supporters' who seemed to be more intent of misbehaving than watching football. During a crowd 'surge' I was pushed down to the floor and had difficulty getting up.

I never went to a football match again.

# CHAPTER NINE

# SCOUTING STANDARDS

Early in 1948 I was asked by Ray Pickering, the Scoutmaster, if I would like to take on the role as treasurer to the 1st Atherstone Scout Troop. 'Mol' Griffiths, the then treasurer and ex-Group Scoutmaster, had expressed a wish to retire if a replacement could be found. Ray had been my Scoutmaster before I had left to join the Air Training Corps in 1942, and had worked very hard to re-build the Troop following his return from Army Service. The Troop was strong but leaders scarce and the Group Committee just about functioning. I took the position willingly and over the next twelve years gradually became more involved in Scouting activities.

By 1961 I had become fully involved. During that year I helped to organise a Gala at Mancetter to try and raise funds for the Atherstone and District International Patrol Camp which was to take place at Hopwas near Tamworth in August. Early the following year I was offered a piece of land on which to build a Scout Headquarters – the scouts had never owned a headquarters of their own, and from their first meeting place of a greenhouse in 1908 when the first patrol was formed under a Mr Tingle, they had met in Church Halls, over a laundry, and, after the 1st and 2nd

Atherstone Groups combined, held all their meetings in the Guide Hut in South Street.

We had been looking for a site for some time, and the committee were holding events with the sole purpose of raising funds to enable the scouts and cubs to eventually have a place of their own. I now took on the role as secretary to a newly-formed Building Sub-Committee. In April we met to decide on the suitability of the site we had been offered. It was about 920 square yards in size with a 48 foot frontage to the main street of the town. I'd managed to negotiate a figure of £400 for the site, which had three-storey terraced houses on it and a fish and chip shop. All the property was condemned and soon to become empty so we decided to buy it although we only had £350 in the bank. It was now April 1962 and for the next two years I became fully involved in arranging for the old property to be demolished, obtaining planning permission for the new building, meetings with our solicitor and bank manager and, most important of all, helping with the money-raising activities and applying for grants which were available for this sort of project. Two and a half years later, just before I left Atherstone and before we'd started on the building, I received confirmation that we had been successful in obtaining almost £2, 000 in grants. The Marley building that was purchased was completed in 1965 and has been the Scout Headquarters ever since. It was a lovely spacious building and a far cry from Mr Tingle's greenhouse of 1908.

Earlier in the January of 1962, Ray had asked me to produce a show that the scouts were putting on in the Parish Room for the parents. I knew nothing about producing a show but I think that he wanted someone who was not involved with the lads to try and get them to make a little more effort, and to put the programme in some sort of order. Little did I know at the time that it was to be the introduction of our involvement into Scout Gang Shows. We put on "These Are The Times" in March for two nights and it was a huge success. Looking back at it now and comparing it with what we were going to do in the following years, it was awful! and not a great improvement on the show in the Guide Hut, which I had taken part in when I had been a scout. At that time I had to show how to tie up a parcel of groceries in order to prevent them from all spilling out when it was being carried. In another sketch, in those early days, a 'newspaper editor' had sat at his desk demanding hot news. Eventually a 'reporter' told him that a man had just shot himself. "When?", asked the editor, fed up with hearing stale news. "Now", said the reporter. There was a loud 'BANG!' as a gun went off, and Pete' Mulford dropped down 'dead'. "Now that's HOT NEWS", said the editor- (End of sketch).

Mrs. Mulford was heard to say a little nervously, "Do you think Peter is alright?" – Twenty years on and we had improved very little.

At Easter I went with the Scouters and the Senior Scouts to North Wales, camping at Mr. Roberts farm at Nantgwnant. On the first day we all did the 'ten-mile-walk', through old slate quarry workings, along a gated road, and across some lovely quiet countryside to Nantmor. The film "The Inn of the Sixth Happiness" was made in this area, and the countryside made to resemble China. Many children from Liverpool's 'Chinatown' came to stay in the villages to work as 'extras' in the film. Now we only had sheep for company as we walked down towards the Aberglaslyn Pass, to join the road which went in the opposite direction to Penryndeudraeth. We rested on the bridge watching the Afon Glaslyn tumbling over the huge boulders of the river bed on its way down to the wide stretches towards Portmadoc, where it joined the sea.

Now level with the river, we made our way alongside the fast flowing waters, balancing ourselves on a long telegraph pole, then hugging a rock as we carefully edged our way round it, and making sure that we kept to the 'path'. Having now reached flatter ground, we crossed a meadow to Beddgelert, occasionally stopping to watch a Dipper dive from his rocky perch into the sparkling clear water of the river, in his search for food.

Nearing this lovely Welsh village in the heart of Snowdonia, we passed Gelert's grave which gave the village its name; Bedd being Welsh for grave. The story goes that in the 13th Century, Llewelyn, Prince of North Wales had a palace here. One day he went out hunting without his faithful hound Gelert, who was unaccountably absent. When Llewelyn returned the dog greeted him joyfully, but the Prince saw that he was stained with blood. Alarmed at this, he went in search of his baby son and saw that his cot was empty, the bedclothes and the floor covered with blood. Llewelyn plunged his sword into the hound's side thinking that the dog had killed his son. The dog's dying yell was answered by the child's cry. The Prince searched and discovered his boy unharmed. Nearby lay the body of a mighty wolf which Gelert had killed in protecting the child. Now filled with remorse for what he had done, it is said that Prince Llewelyn never smiled again and buried Gelert here.

No one knows whether the story is true but the village has many visitors, most of whom visit Gelert's grave, who hope that it is.

Having called in one of a number of cafes for a welcome cup of tea we carried on along the side of the river, skirted Llyn Dinas and then on to the narrow road which led to our camp site. We always regarded the ten-mile-walk as a 'loosener' before tackling the much more challenging and strenuous climbs of the surrounding mountains; Moel Hebog, Cnicht, and some of the ones over three thousand feet, Glyder Fawr, Glyder Fach, Tryfan and, of course, the Snowdon Horseshoe.

Next day we climbed Snowdon on the Watkin Path, passing the Gladstone Rock inscribed with details in both Welsh and English, commemorating the statesman's visit in 1892. At this spot, 1000ft above sea level, and when he was 84 years of age, he addressed the Welsh Nation on 'Freedom for the Small States'. Seldom had so many people gathered together on the slopes of Snowdon.

This Easter Camp was my first introduction to the mountains of North Wales and I loved every minute of it. I was to climb most of the other routes to the top of Snowdon in later years, and on three occasions the whole Horseshoe – Crib-goch, Crib-y-ddysal, Snowdon, Y Lliwedd, then down to Llyn Llydaw to join the Miner's Track and back to the starting point at Pen-y-pass.

I was never happier than mountain walking in Snowdonia and experiencing the thrill and excitement of reaching 'the top' to enjoy the spectacular views. Hands were seldom wanted during the climbs except on Tryfan and possibly the Crib-goch ridge.

In 1862, George Borrow in his book 'Wild Wales', maybe overstated the case when he wrote, "Perhaps in the whole world there is no region more picturesquely beautiful than Snowdon, a region of mountains, lakes, cataracts and groves, in which nature shows herself in her most grand and beautiful form." Nevertheless, there are many people who would agree with him and who keep returning to walk the routes of Snowdonia time and time again. We once saw two ladies, well into their 70s, walking on the difficult Aberglaslyn footpath to Beddgelert. Next day, after we had climbed the PYG (Pen-y-Gwryd) route on Snowdon, we met them again near to the top. They had walked the very long route all the way from Llanberis but were hoping to return on the Snowdon Railway. They looked considerably fitter and less exhausted after their climb than our small party of young scouts.

Soon after we returned from that Easter camp I started some research into the beginning of scouting in Atherstone and chatted with some of the old scouts who had been in the first patrol under the leadership of Mr Tingle. I discovered that sometime in 1908 less than a dozen scouts had held their first meeting in the converted greenhouse at the rear of a house in Owen Street, under the leadership of Eustace M. Tingle who was later to become the local Army Recruiting Officer for Atherstone during the 'Great War'.

The troop had included among others Harry Mills, Dick Archer, Fred Rice, Tom Lockley, Ted Comley, 'Piddy' Deeming, Horace Love, Jack Tingle and Jack Summers who were all members of the

'Adder' patrol. As the numbers had grown, indoor activities had taken place in the Parish Room in Welcome Street. They then had moved the headquarters to Sheepy Road into the coach houses belonging to Atherstone Hall, and later another move had been made to the room over Albert Wainwright's carpenters workshop opposite the Parish Church of St. Mary's.

Some of the activities had been based on military games one of which was 'Flag-Raiding' in the Outwoods by day, and also at night with the aid of a lamp. Sentries had guarded the centre whilst the 'enemy' had crept up from the surrounding area either to capture the flag or put out the light. Quickly the numbers had grown to over 100 including 'Navvy' Griffiths, Bill'Reynard'Fox, Charlie'Cleo'Ford, 'Chips'Harrison the bugler, and Tom Burke who was later killed in the 1914-18 War.

I was told that competitions had taken place against other troops in the district and one of the most popular had entailed getting a dispatch through to a particular Post Office and having it stamped by various Post Offices on the way. On one occasion Dick Archer had taken the message on foot to Nuneaton and had hidden the message in the lining of his shoe. Later the game had been played over longer distances by bicycle, and once in Birmingham, having carried the dispatch via Coleshill, he had seen another troop's message sewn inside a herring!

Pathfinding and tracking had also been popular and entailed laying false trails. This would often take them many miles astray, even as far as Shustoke, seven miles from Atherstone. One evening, Jack Summers, hot on the trail at Pinwall, had used his staff to leap over a pigsty and landed 'flop' into the pig trough.

In his publication of 'Scouting for Boys', Baden Powell wrote a 'Yarn', as he called his chapters, on 'Saving Life' and stressed the importance of knowing what to do and doing it at once. The boys were constantly on the lookout for situations which might present themselves where they could put this into action. 'Piddy' Deeming had once jumped fully clothed into the river at Grendon Hall to 'save' another scout from drowning. As 'Piddy' was then excused from going on that morning's Church Parade – everyone did their best to get out of going to those – there had been a slight suspicion amongst the other scouts as to whether the boy had really needed to be 'saved', but Mr Tingle had had no doubts and recommended him for an award which he had received in the form of a parchment scroll.

There was another story about a scout who had been out on a pathfinding activity and on hearing a scream succeeded in surprising a man who was apparently molesting a girl. Upon receiving no satisfactory answer to his questions, he had promptly delivered a 'staggering blow to the chin', knocking the man off his feet, which at the time had been regarded as a very brave and courageous thing to do, considering that the scout in question was normally of a gentle nature. However, Mr Tingle had made no recommendation for an award in this instance, much to the disappointment of the boy who thought that he had least saved the girl's honour if not her life! For many years after that he was known as 'Staggering blow to the chin Archer'.

Tom Lockley was another scout to react quickly to a dramatic situation, and this time his alertness and promptness of action certainly saved a man's life. In a later edition of 'Scouting for Boys', in Camp Yarn 24 on 'Accidents and How to Deal with Them' the account of what happened is dramatically chronicled by Baden Powell.

"Scout Lockley of the 1st Atherstone Troop was looking on at a round-about at a fair which was being worked by electricity from a steam traction engine. The driver of this on leaning over got his clothes caught in the machinery and was being dragged into it, when Lockley sprang on to the engine and knowing something of mechanics, pulled the lever and stopped it just in time to save a man's life". The passage concluded – "Here is an example of a fellow

Being Prepared – knowing what to do, and doing it without a moment's waiting".

Tom Lockley had been presented with the Silver Medal given by General Baden Powell, as he was known then, and the presentation was made at the Parish Room in November 1909 by Mr J. E. Compton Bracebridge who was later made District Commissioner of Scouts.

While I was doing this research I wondered whether Tom was still alive. I discovered that he had been killed in an air-raid in Nuneaton during the war but his widow still had the medal as well as the parchment scroll rolled up in a drawer. She gave me the scroll and we had it framed to hang up in the new headquarters when it was built. One of the rooms in the building was named the 'Lockley Room' and she also gave the Silver Medal to the Group later for safe keeping, an act of generosity and thoughtfulness that has enabled this piece of local scout history to be preserved.

This first scout troop had planned to walk to Windsor for the 1911 Review by King George V but had had second thoughts and had gone by train, and there joined the other 26, 000 scouts who had assembled. The King had dismounted from his horse to walk round the troop and had asked Tom Lockley about the significance of the ribbons on the flag staff he had been holding. Previously there had been a great uproar in the arena when the Union Jack was raised on the flag pole: Mr Tingle always maintained that it had been the Lion Patrol who had been the first to 'boo' when it was noticed that the flag was upside down, and the incident was referred to for many years as 'the roar of the Lions'! The Atherstone Town Band had met the boys at the railway station on their return and they had marched along Long Street to the Red Lion Hotel.

In 1915 members of the troop had included Tom Stafford, Alf Webster, Alec Evans, Eric Hatton, Spen Hatton, George Gilbert, Harry Mills, Clem Johnson, Tom Lockley and his brother, and other boys named Tillson, Webster and Cowlishaw. This then had been the beginning of Scouting in Atherstone in 1908.

In September 1962 I went back into uniform to help Gordon Webster with the Senior Scout Troop. They met in a 'Den' over the top of some garages at "Oakfields", a large house and grounds in Arden Hill belonging to Mrs Vero who was a supporter and good friend of scouting in Atherstone. They were a nice group of lads and one in particular, John Caswell, worked very hard to try and obtain his Queen's Scout Award. He managed to get it and went to Windsor with other Queen Scouts for the St George's Day Parade in 1963.

We were all very proud of him. Sadly he was killed a few years later while mountaineering in Scotland.

On one of those Snowdon 'horseshoe' climbs at one Easter week-end, we witnessed two incidents which unfortunately occur too frequently on mountains. The first was when a young girl 'froze' on the Crib-goch ridge. We were eventually able to persuade her to move and prevent her companions from taking her down the wrong way, then soon afterwards, we saw a man fall as he descended Crib-y-ddysal. We were the first to get to him. He was badly injured and saved from falling any further since he lay in a cleft in the rock face. Later he was lifted off the mountain by helicopter and taken to hospital. The sole of his boot was loose, which had probably caused him to lose his footing. There's a true saying that, "Mountains are not dangerous – it's the people who are on them who are dangerous!" We often found this to be true and always took great care to ensure that the lads in our charge obeyed the 'rules' of mountain walking. E. G. Rowland gives excellent advice in his book 'Hill Walking in Snowdonia' – essential reading for all those who contemplate tackling the mountains of North Wales – and I believe that if his advice had been followed by the majority of the people involved in accidents on mountains, many of the tragedies that have occurred all too frequently, could have been avoided.

However, on one occasion at an Easter Camp we almost lost

three scouts due mainly to the severe weather conditions at the time. Gordon and I eventually found them in a very desolate area, trudging along on the route we had given them through the rocks and the heather in Cwm Edno. We hadn't anticipated that the ground would have become so boggy due to the constant rain and as the weather was so bad and the ground getting worse, we took them back to the road where they then had to walk six or seven miles to the camp site carrying their hike tent and all their equipment. The rain continued all Saturday night blowing a fine spray through the canvas, so next day we were forced to strike camp in driving rain and head back home with all our equipment, clothes and sleeping bags soaked. On the Easter Monday the sun shone fiercely from a clear blue sky!

During the winter of 1962-63, Gordon and I organised a night hike in response to the lads' request for a challenging adventure. On a snowy evening, we sent them off in two groups towards Bentley and arranged for us all to meet later. The snow fell relentlessly, paths through the woods disappeared and wrong routes taken. When we did eventually all meet in the early hours – much later than we had planned – we found it impossible to melt the snow on our small paraffin stove to enable us to make a hot drink. According to reports the next day, it turned out to be the coldest night in living memory – even the anti-freeze in car radiators froze!

In the following March (of 1963) the Scouters and wives went to Coventry to see the Gang Show performed by Coventry Scouts at the College Theatre. It was reputed to be one of the best in the country and modelled on the Ralph Reader Shows which he wrote and produced each year at the Odeon Theatre, Golders Green. The Coventry Show included some of their own ideas including a Cub number which almost stole the show. After a visit back-stage and a chat with the producers, we were confident that we could put one on in Atherstone. After my 'success' with 'These are the Times', Ray appointed me producer, and the Scoutmaster and his wife June took on the task of organising the costumes. We realised that we couldn't possibly do a full scale Scout Show without help from outside the Movement – we were very small in numbers compared to Coventry – and that we would have to perform it on a full size stage in the new Memorial Hall.

Ray gave me a book to read, written by Ralph Reader, on how to put on a Gang Show. I made notes and plans of what we needed to do and, after consulting the other Scouters, invited everyone I knew that might be able to help, to a meeting in the Guide Hut. We told them that we would be putting on a Show lasting about two-and-a-half hours with seventy scouts and cubs and eight girl guides. There would be eighteen musical numbers and sketches which would involve over two-hundred-and-fifty changes of costume. Our Show would run for three nights in January and we planned to start rehearsals in September. I explained that we were looking for help with make-up, dressing the cast, back-stage, lighting, refreshments for both the public and cast, and house management. Everyone listened in silence, and in a state of incredulity. The representatives from the Amateur Dramatic Society (used to three-act plays with few, if any, changes of costume) thought we couldn't possibly be serious but finally agreed to help.

Although we took the shows very seriously, we all had a tremendous amount of fun. Team spirit was very much in evidence throughout the performances with everyone striving to do their best. The Cub Numbers – produced by the Cub Scouters – were a delight, and included satirical versions of 'Camelot' and 'Babes in the Wood'. The lads seemed to show no stage nerves in performing for the first time in front of an audience and enjoyed dressing up. "Call of the Open Road" where cubs were dressed as brownies and scouts as guides, was a show stopper, and cries of "Where's my skirt?" were often heard in the dressing room under the stage.

One of the numbers we had planned to do in the show involved the Scout Hymn, but the only recording we had was on a brittle

78rpm record which got broken. We then discovered that the record was unobtainable and were left with only a printed copy of the words and music.

The plan for the number had been to have someone explaining the significance of the Scout Badge, a scout reciting the Scout Laws and another scout taking his Promise. All this, together with the Scout Hymn playing in the background, was to be recorded on tape, and mimed on stage. It was to be the only serious number in the show, and a contrast to all the other humorous sketches and musical numbers, so if we were still to do it, we knew that we would have to make our own recording of the hymn, one way or another.

We enlisted the help of Richard Margoschis, a local recording expert, and Jack Coles, our Musical Director, who was also the organist and Choirmaster at the Congregational Church. Sitting in the front row of the church pews, I gave the signal to bring the choir and each person in at the precise moment, as Richard adjusted the volume of the different microphones as he made the recording.

"Now as I go upon my Chosen way,
In all I do, my thoughts, my work, my play,
Grant as I promise, Courage new for me
To be the best, the best that I can be."

As the rich baritone voice of Mr Jones sang the first verse as a solo, the curtain opened slowly revealing the huge shining silver badge in a spotlight, and then the spoken voice:-
. . . . . "This is our badge. . ."

It was a great success each night, and so was the show which we called, 'It's a Wonderful Life" and played to full houses. Encouraged by what we had achieved, we did an even better one the following year, this time for a week, entitled "Would You Believe It?" and a third two years later in 1967, "You're Only Young Once". We were not allowed to call them' Gang Shows' until we had Ralph Reader's approval and had performed a minimum of three shows to a good standard and on a full stage. This we considered we had now done and, soon afterwards, the 'Gang' were awarded the coveted 'Red Scarf' of the Gang Show which they wore on future performances after I had left. Meanwhile, the Scout Band was beginning to reach high standards too, and achieved good positions in the National Scout Band Championships. These two events gave the Scout Movement in the district an enormous upsurge in popularity and support.

During this time, the Scout Movement nationally was going through many changes. The Chief Scout, Sir Charles Maclean, had formed an Advance Party... "to study all aspects of the future of Scouting and to make recommendations". They produced 409 of them. Although most dealt with the development of the Movement, the one that seemed to receive the most publicity from outside the organisation was Recommendation 253.

"That in future shorts only be worn as standard uniform by Cub Scouts; all other boys and men in the Movement to wear long trousers".

This, together with some of the more radical changes, was too much for some of the old traditional Scouters who threatened to continue with Scouting as laid down by Baden Powell. At our own Warwickshire County Annual Conference at Solihull, for instance, one Scouter turned up in shorts, when in previous years he had gone against the traditional uniform, and worn long trousers! The plans for the future were adventurous and much more challenging and in keeping with the changed attitude of young people.

Also for the first time, the Aim and Method of the Movement was laid down in Recommendation 2:-

(a) "The aim of the Scout Association is to encourage the physical, mental and spiritual development of young people so that they may take a constructive place in society".

(b) "The method of achieving the aim of the Association is by providing an enjoyable and attractive scheme of progressive training, based on the Scout Law and Promise and guided by leadership".

There was also a recommendation that all Scouters should be called 'leaders'. The Patrol system, which was revolutionary as a method of training when first introduced by Baden Powell in his 'Scouting for Boys' was, of course, to be retained and strengthened. We noted that Recommendation 306 stated:-

"That while Gang Shows continue, every effort be made to ensure that the highest possible standard be maintained".

We hoped that we were already complying with this recommendation.

In September 1964, the Pearl moved me to the Burton-on-Trent Office. Although I still travelled back and forth to Atherstone to do the second and third shows, I took on the position of Group Scout Leader of the 18th Burton (Stretton)Group. It proved to be quite a challenge. The Cub Pack had a number of leaders but the Troop hadn't, and the standard of scouting was low. However, there was a strong Group Committee of parents – redesignated as 'Group Council' in the APR – and soon I was able to obtain the services of two Scouters living in the village, to run the troop. We had summer camps in Wales, Scotland and Germany as well as England, during the six or seven years I was with the Group. With the committee's help, we organised money-raising activities, including Cheese and Wine Evenings and Garden-Fetes, to enable us to purchase tents and camping equipment.

Camping was great fun, and whether I was organising a Scout camp or just taking part, I enjoyed the freedom of the outdoor life. The memories of days under canvas are unforgettable: good companionship and conversation late into the evening around what had been earlier a camp fire, and in the morning, as one lay warm inside a sleeping bag, the sounds of the dawn chorus heralding a new day. Then on with plimsoles, (no socks) and a run through the dewy grass to the stream for a wash, returning to cook breakfast over an open fire as the early sunlight filtered through the trees of a nearby wood. The sounds of laughter confirmed that the boys too enjoyed the life outdoors with their pals, some of whom had previously only experienced the discipline of a boarding-house or small hotel with their Mum and Dad.

Camp-fires in the evening sometimes began with the words of Rudyard Kipling.

"Who hath smelt woodsmoke at twilight?
Who hath heard the birch log burning?
Who is quick to read the noises of the night?
Let him follow with the others,
For the young men's feet are turning
To the camps of proved desire and known delight."

The summer camp when we took the troop to the continent in 1970 was, however, something special. The seven months previous to departure saw a gradual process of planning, discussion, letters to Germany, Belgium and Luxembourg, assembling equipment, hiring mini-buses, booking ferries, working out menus, and estimating the cost for a two week camp. We also arranged for someone to give the lads German lessons on troop nights and completed the itinerary and timetable. Finally we purchased the traveller's cheques, foreign currency, maps, passports, tickets, badges, and the food we were to take with us. We loaded the three Volkswagen vehicles, settled the passengers and the parents waved us off. After a night's stay in a Scout Headquarters in Hendon, and a pleasant Channel crossing next morning, we were soon bumping along the uneven roads of France, then on to the wide dual carriageways of Belgium to our next overnight stop south of Namur. Crossing the German border on Sunday morning, we left our four Venture Scouts on the outskirts of Cologne with their hike tents. They were to rejoin us in Luxembourg a week later.

We reached our camp site that afternoon along a narrow wooded valley at Bendorf-Sayn. The winding road ran alongside a fast-moving stream, crossed at every other bend by high-arched railway bridges almost obscured by the trees. Every hour or so, clouds of white smoke billowed through the tops of the trees as the trains puffed up or down the single track, much to the delight of the railway enthusiasts. On the wider bends, tents of all shapes and sizes covered the grassy meadows. Scouts and Guides from Germany, Belgium, Holland, France and Great Britain, joined together throughout the week to make it a wonderful occasion of international scouting.

The following Sunday we were in Luxembourg on a much smaller site at Echternach, where we met up with our Venture Scouts. They had spent one night with us at Bendorf but I think had spent more time at wine festivals than doing the projects we'd set them on their journey down the Rhine and Mosel! We arranged a visit to Luxembourg City for those wishing to go before setting off later in the week on the long journey home. The total cost per head for the thirty-two of us, was less than twenty pounds for the two weeks.

I think the best memories for most of us were the camp-fires at Bendorf: the sweet harmony of the Guide songs, the humour of the German sketches, the originality of the talented Belgian instrumental group, and the friendly way that a hundred Guides approached our camp fire, hand-in-hand in a snake like procession, singing as they came. Then there was the dancing by the Dutch Guides, lit only by the flickering flames of the fire, the rocket display by the German Scouts, and everyone linking hands at the Belgian Camp-fire singing "Auld Lang Syne", some in their own language.

We all enjoyed the trip in the mini-buses to Rudesheim in glorious sunshine and the next day's trip on the Rhine to St.Goar, the return trip highlighted by a friendly elderly German giving the lads the history of the castles and explaining to them the ancient techniques which are still used in the vineyards today. He described how the broken slate which was placed around and beneath the vines not only prevented erosion on the steep sides of the Rhine and Mosel valleys, but kept the soil moist and reflected the sun to the underside of the grapes enabling them to ripen evenly on the vines.

Most of the lads enjoyed the hike in mid-week organised by the Camp Chief, Hans Brog, when Scouts and Guides from the five countries hiked together for over three hours through the pine woods to a village, and then caught the train to take them back which stopped specially for them at the camp site. One of the requirements for the 'Advanced Scout Standard' award was to "complete a twelve mile journey on foot, camping overnight with a scout of your own age, and produce a written account of your journey". Two of the lads would not easily forget where they had completed their journey – along the banks of the Rhine between Rudesheim and St.Goarshausen. They would always remember these days of scout comradeship – as we all would – and in the words of one of Ralph Reader's Gang Show song
"When the years have rolled away
We shall dream of the times we've had,
The songs we used to sing,
But while we're together, let us laugh at the weather
Whatever the gods may bring.
When all our youth is but memories
And the years bring parting of the ways
Then these are the times we shall dream about
And we'll call them the good old days".

As soon as I had completed the last Atherstone show, I asked the District Commissioner in Burton-on-Trent if I could do one there. The result was that I did three District Shows, bigger and more ambitious than previously: "Three Cheers" in 1968, "Crest of a Wave" in 1969, and the final one in 1971 with the same title. I was well supported by other Scouters in the District and we achieved a very high standard, helped enormously by the professionalism of our Musical Director, Hartley Mallinson. I then left Scouting temporarily at the end of 1971 and didn't go back into the Movement until six years later when I moved to Boston. Meanwhile, the shows continued in Burton and they too were awarded the 'Red

Scarf' like Atherstone.

Looking now for an easy life, I accepted an invitation to be Group Scout leader of a well-run and successful Group at Butterwick, the 10th Boston. I should have known better. The Scout leader, who had been running the Troop for many years left to take up the appointment of Assistant District Commissioner (Scouts). Then both the Assistant Scout leaders left for different reasons, and I found myself again running a Troop practically on my own, but I did have excellent Cub Scout leaders and a good Group Council in support.

Fortunately the Patrol Leaders had been well trained and the troop had a long tradition of winning or doing well, in District Cooking or Camping competitions, which they continued to do. Some of the lads also competed in the National Scout Go-Kart Championships and one of the Scouters who had left continued to keep an interest in this sport, taking them to the events and supervising the building of the vehicles. Some of the older boys also took part in 'Parascending' at a disused airfield near Grantham and did extremely well. After six years in Boston, the Pearl transferred me to Grimsby and I left Scouting for good in 1983. I was now 55 and I had first joined as a cub when I was 8 years old.

Scouting had been fun: I'd enjoyed every minute of it and made many friends, but I'd had enough. Over the years we had many a discussion as to why we did it. Someone once suggested that we were only boys who refused to grow up, or maybe it was that we wanted to give to the present generation the fun that we had had out of Scouting when we had been their age. Whatever the reasons, I don't believe many of us ever gave thought to any 'sense of duty', or had any particular moral or honourable motivations. We did, however, always treat the Scout Promise seriously and not only taught the boys the importance of it but tried to live by it ourselves. The Advance Party recommended that the expression 'On my honour' should be deleted from it as it was 'no longer in common use', but when it was, I believe it lost something. In the early days we used to ask a scout before he took his promise, if he knew what his honour meant. He would reply:

"Yes, it means that I can be trusted to be truthful and honest." With the Report, that went out and we were left with:

(On my honour).."I promise that I will do my best, to do my duty to God, and to the Queen – To help other people and to keep the Scout Law."

It always saddened me to know that owing to a perpetual shortage of leaders, most Cub Packs had a waiting list and some boys were never able to join the Movement. Others often made sure they didn't miss out: I recall a story told to me of one boy who put his name down when he was only 6 years old. He went again when he was 7 but was told that he couldn't join until the obligatory age of 8. The very day he was to celebrate his 8th birthday coincided with Cub night. His mother informed 'Akela' (Cub Leader), that he wouldn't be able to join that week after all as he would be having his birthday party. But Jimmy knew better. He contacted all his friends, postponed the party until next day and turned up as he had planned two years earlier. Sometimes Akelas never realised how important they were! Another story was told to me by a Scouter who had been travelling in his car listening to the local radio, when he was suddenly aware of a small child's voice talking to the disc-jockey over the telephone. It was one of those programmes when the presenter invited housewives to ring in and tell him whom they loved best and why, and obviously he was surprised to hear such a young voice.

"And who are you?" he asked.

"Richard".

"Richard who?" "Thompson".

"And where do you Live, Richard?" "Number 9".

It was one of those one-sided coversations that could have gone on all day,

Eventually he came to the crux question.

"And whom do you love best?"

"Akela".

There was a moment's silence. You could almost hear the presenter saying,

"Who the bl—y hell's Akela?" – He restrained himself:

"And who is that, Richard?"

"Our Cub leader".

"And why do you love her the best?"

"Because she talks to me!"

You see", said my friend, "he'd explained that he had a number of brothers and sisters older than himself and perhaps no one had time for him. He hadn't said he'd loved his mother best or anyone else in the family, he had to tell someone he loved Akela because she talked to him, and what's more he'd beaten about 50,000 housewives to the telephone to do so....and we worry about whether we should be in long trousers or shorts!"

I wonder whether that Scouter who came to the Warwickshire County Conference ever heard that story?!

# CHAPTER TEN

# SHAKING THE SHACKLES

I spent many hours getting very wet on my bicycle as I travelled around the district doing my collecting. Usually I went out prepared for the worst as we had no reliable long term weather forecasting to go by, and relied on our own early morning observations as to what the weather would do later in the day. I was caught out, though, more than once and often came home after a day calling in the villages in the country with the pockets in my coat soaking and the coins inside all stuck together. If the day had seen me writing some new business however, I felt good whatever my personal discomfort.

I only had one serious misfortune on my cycle. It was Monday morning, the start of a new week, and raining, and I set off at the beginning of a long day along the Watling Street to Mancetter. There was very little traffic and I remember a van overtaking me. Keeping my head down against the driving rain, I glanced up now and again to see if the road was clear ahead. Too late! – the van had stopped outside the school and I was within six feet of its rear doors. Fortunately I was only bruised, but left with a tangled heap of buckled tubing and a twisted front wheel for my only means of transport. I carried it back to Farmer's Cycle shop and borrowed another until mine was repaired. A few years later I decided to purchase a New Hudson Auto-cycle for which I paid about £75. Although it enabled me to cover my area much more quickly, therefore reducing the time I spent collecting, I missed the peaceful and natural sounds of the countryside. I was now frightening away with my noisy machine, the birds and animals which I had often seen when I was on my bike: The yellow-hammer sitting on the top of a hawthorn hedge singing his easily recognisable 'little-bit-of-bread-and-no-cheese' song; the sudden sighting of the magnificently-coloured male bull-finch; the occasional fox or small animal scurrying along the road, or in the case of a hedgehog, trotting along hurriedly until it saw me approach then curling up into a ball for protection. During the winter I would come across charms of gold-finches or a small flock of long-tailed tits flitting from tree to tree with perhaps a tree-creeper for company.

The little three-wheeler I then bought gave me a lot more comfort, keeping me dry and warm in the severe weather and the soft top, which folded back, allowing me still to enjoy the open air life. The front wheel was chain-driven by the 198cc Villiers engine mounted above it, and could turn a full 90% either way, enabling the car to face the opposite direction by pivoting on one of the back wheels. I tried this manoeuvre in a quiet country lane on my first day out with the vehicle, but suddenly came face to face with an old Austin Seven. Unfortunately I panicked, pressed down on the accelerator pedal instead of the brake, and as I crashed into him a cloud of rusty dust, all from the old Austin, rose into the air. When it cleared I saw that the other car was being driven by a fellow insurance man whom I knew. As no serious damage was done we had a good laugh about it. He told me that he couldn't believe his eyes when he suddenly saw me do a complete reverse turn on the spot and then come straight for him. My number plate was broken, but his old car had so many dents, scratches and rusty parts, that we couldn't decide what damage I had caused (if any) and what had been there before.

On one occasion the front wheel came off whilst doing about 35 miles per hour, and acting like a cushion, it jammed itself underneath the engine protecting it from any further damage. The car slid along the road for a number of yards, until coming to rest on a grassy bank. Apart from a new tyre, only the wheel bolts needed to be replaced, and the bodywork of the car was undamaged. On another occasion as I went over the humped-back bridge over the river Anker on the way to Ratcliffe Culey the bonnet flew off: again no damage to me, just a lot of scratched paintwork.

The most serious accident happened when I wasn't even in the vehicle. I was about to get into the car when I saw a lorry coming towards me travelling rather fast. I moved away just before another lorry that he was towing sliced down the side of my car, tossing it across the pavement with bits of the fibre-glass body flying up into the air. When I changed the vehicle I kept my fingers crossed in case anything else happened to it while waiting for my new mini-van to be delivered. On the last day I could smell smoke as I was driving through the town; I stopped and called someone over to look under the bonnet as I ran the engine.

"There's no smoke here", my fellow citizen informed me, putting his head right inside the car – bravely I thought, as it could have blown up as I sat safely behind the wheel!

"Well there's plenty of smoke in here", I replied, a little hysterically, and then, beginning to feel warm, realised that I'd put my pipe in my pocket and my jacket was on fire!

I made a lot of friends in the seventeen years I called on people, and shared their joys and their sorrows. I was often taken into their confidence and my advice sought on many occasions. I was asked to witness signatures on wills and many other documents, and became quite adept in filling in tax forms for my policyholders. I also was often asked to explain the new legislation in the Industrial Insurance Act of 1948 and who would be entitled to the new government death benefits introduced in the Act.

I listened patiently, sometimes in discreet silence, to gossip, personal ailments and family grievances, and (thankfully on rare occasions) became involved in marital disagreements.

"What do you think about a man who spends all his money on horses?"

I was once asked by a disgruntled farmer's wife in front of her husband, who rode regularly with the Atherstone Hounds. At the time I was canvassing their two sons and daughter to take out an endowment policy each.

"The boys can't afford it – he doesn't pay them enough wages", she added, pointing her finger accusingly at her husband but still looking at me – "spends all his money on horses", she repeated.

"Well perhaps you could start them off by paying the premiums for them for a while", I suggested, searching for a way out of the difficult situation.

"Of course I will", he said throwing me his cheque book. He'd replied immediately, anxious to show his wife and me that he wasn't as mean as she had made him out to be. The farmer's wife gave me a wry smile from behind her husband's back and left the room. I suddenly realised that I'd been involved in a conspiracy, but I was happy to walk away with three proposals and a cheque for the first premiums.

I took a visiting inspector to a neighbouring farm and by the time he had reached the farmhouse, after driving along the track through a couple of fields where a Friesian herd was grazing, he had worked out the amount of the farmer's monthly milk cheque from the Milk Marketing Board. This gave the inspector an idea of what sort of premium the farmer would be able to afford, but on this occasion we weren't able to sell him any life assurance. I enjoyed doing business with farmers. They were quick to see the tax advantages of Deferred Annuity policies (the forerunner of Personal Pensions) and were always interested in a good anticipated return for their outlay – rather like expecting a good crop after sowing I thought. A handshake concluded the business and then they would always hand me their cheque book for me to write out the cheque.

That same trust and handshake could be seen at the Tuesday Cattle Market in Station Street, and then one knew that a deal had been done although nothing was signed. Their word was their bond. I went there whenever I could and it was fascinating to watch the auctioneer, John Briggs, picking up the bids quickly, and not missing a nod of the head, wink or the lifting on a finger from the crowd around him – mostly farmers he knew well. The sharp tap of his pencil on his book completed every sale as the calves and heifers exchanged hands.

Some of the farmers were members of the Atherstone Hunt and rode regularly with them. I had business with the people at the kennels in Witherley village and although most of the hounds looked identical to me, the Whippers-in knew them all by name. I enjoyed the spectacle of the Meet, with the Huntsmen in their 'Pinks' and the Whippers-in in full control of the hounds. I held no particular view of fox-hunting which began in the late 17th century as a practical method of limiting the fox population, and at that time endangered poultry farming. Later the British aristocracy and gentry ceremonialized it and treated it as a sport, which prompted Oscar Wilde to describe it as "the unspeakable in pursuit of the uneatable". I knew it as a winter outing for farmers, those who 'spent all their money on horses' and one didn't think about the possible cruelty to the beautiful fox.

On one occasion, however, I was a little too close to the action for comfort. Cycling along a narrow country lane to a farm in the village of Atterton, I heard a hunting-horn and immediately in front of me a fox suddenly appeared. We both stopped, looked at each other for a second or two and then he sped off across the fields. I pedalled quickly away as the dogs squeezed through the fence and hedge in pursuit of their prey, closely followed by the horses and riders. They rode off in the direction of Fenny Drayton, another small Leicestershire village, which is famous for a different sort of fox altogether. This is George Fox, English founder of the Society of Friends (Quakers), and by the side of the road in the village where he was born in 1624, stood a small memorial to him. The deserted Lindley Aerodrome, (later to be the home of MIRA) a mile or so from Fenny Drayton had been occupied by squatters after the war and the huts converted by the local authority into acceptable dwellings for the homeless. It was one of the areas where I called on Friday nights, and I was pleased when people were re-housed and the war time nissen huts demolished.

During the first few years my average weekly life assurance collections amounted to about £48, all in cash, plus a few quarterly payments and small yearly amounts for non-life business. The only cheques I was given were from farmers, doctors, schoolteachers and businessmen. I recall only one housewife during that time who paid me by cheque. When I went to take her the proceeds of her policy at the maturity date, she told me that she and her friend had both taken out a 20 year endowment at the same time and had made plans to celebrate when the policies matured, but sadly her friend had died a few years later.

I naturally preferred paying out maturity proceeds but also realised the importance of dealing promptly with claims when people died. A poor family who had been re-housed from one of the 'yards' in the 1930's were still paying the one penny infantile policies which they had taken out when their children had been born, thirty years or forty years ago. They had been so grateful for the sum assured paid to them when one of their babies had died in the 1920's. It had been sufficient to cover the funeral expenses of about five or six pounds. Even in the ten years or so after the Second World War few people still had sufficient savings to cover funeral expenses without causing hardship, and relied on assurance policies, but as the people began to have better-paid jobs and became more prosperous, they started to save by taking out larger endowment policies, some utilising them for house purchase.

Sometimes an unusual situation or happening would occur which made people aware of the need to take out additional life assurance or insurance cover. One tragic accident occurred in 1950 at Creswell Colliery in Derbyshire with over 200 men killed or injured, which had a profound effect on the mining community in Atherstone. This resulted in a number of miners increasing the amount of their life cover. Another situation of a lighter nature happened at Market Bosworth Show, held in the Hall grounds of the Dixie family who had been around this Leicestershire Market Town for over 300 years. The show was very popular, with the usual livestock judging and agricultural events in the morning, followed by cycle racing and a gymkhana in the afternoon. Someone won a coconut at the fair, and in a moment of irresponsibility we began throwing it to each other in the area where the cars were parked. Soon the inevitable happened when it fell on to the bonnet of a car, denting it.

"Can you insure for this sort of thing?" one of my friends asked, rather concerned at what he had done and the probable cost involved. I explained the position briefly and later completed two proposals for Personal Liability Insurances for a premium of ten-shillings a year each. When I subsequently collected the renewal premiums, we always referred to them as 'Coconut Insurances!'

Market Bosworth is, of course, associated with the Battle of Bosworth in 1485 (the last battle of the Wars of the Roses) although it actually took place on Redmore Plain nearer to Sutton Cheney and Stoke Golding. A mural depicting the battle is on the wall behind the bar of "The Three Tuns" in Atherstone's Long Street, and when I called on the landlord of this inn, reputedly near to where Henry (Earl of Richmond) had stayed the night, it was easy to imagine this being the place – true or not – where he met with the Stanleys to discuss the strategy of the conflict which was to take place a few miles away a couple of days later.

Lord Stanley, who had previously been loyal to Richard 111, was reluctant to join with Henry openly, due to the fact that his son Lord Strange, was held by the King as a traitor. However, it appears that Stanley had brought his army through Atherstone to camp a little ahead of Henry's army which was camped at Merevale Abbey on the Saturday night, August 20th. Henry met with Lord Stanley and his brother Sir William on that day, when he also consulted with Sir John Savage, Sir Brian Sanford, Sir Simon Digby and many others, all deserters from King Richard. Before the Battle, Henry took the Sacrament in the church of an Augustinian Friary which was almost certain to have become St. Mary's Parish Church after the dissolution of the monasteries.

The landlord of "The Three Tuns", Cornelius Hill, had also previously been an agent for the Pearl at Polesworth under the Tamworth Office, and he described to me how in the 1930's he carried a small bottle of ink in his waistcoat pocket into which he would dip his pen. It made me appreciate having the use of a fountain pen.

One of my unusual calls was to the Convent behind a high wall on the outskirts of Atherstone. I was always amused as I stood before the high door of the grey stone building and grasped the handle, pulling down on a long metal rod which disappeared into the roof of the porch above me. Instead of the loud clanging of a bell which one would have expected, and no doubt had happened many years earlier, there was a soft 'bzzzz' from the electric buzzer to which it was now connected.

Early on the evening of 22nd November 1963 I called at a house in Ansley Common, and as the lady opened the door she spoke the words that were to be said by millions of people on that Friday.

"Kennedy's been shot!"

A few more calls later I learnt that he was dead. I went home.

As President of the United States, he had been only a young man among a lot of much older world leaders, and as was said by many people of many nations, with his assassination "a light had gone out in the world". Most of us still remember where we were and what we were doing when the news came through from Dallas. As a mark of respect and in memory of the US President who had been killed so violently, crowds stood for a minute's silence at football grounds throughout the country before their matches next day.

I called at a house in the village of Sheepy Magna, often greeted by an elderly lady who lived with her niece. She seemed to be always sitting upright in her chair, hands together in her lap, her greying hair tied in a bun behind her head. Although pleasant, I never saw her smile and she told me that she had studied Spiritualism under Arthur Conan Doyle when she lived in Leicester. Also a clairvoyant, she once told me that someone was trying to influence me from 'the other side'.

"He's an old man with white hair and has a walking stick – do you know who I mean?" she asked looking at me, knowingly. I suppose it sounded very much like my grandpa who had died some years earlier, but possibly a large percentage of the population had had a grandfather who fitted that description! Without waiting for my answer she added,

"He's telling you to 'shake the shackles' – and you're going to move away".

I knew that wasn't true as I'd only recently turned down an offer of promotion to go and work at a District in the Birmingham area. However, "shaking the shackles" made me think what I was doing with my life and whether I was entrenched in too many other things at the expense of my career.

I had become increasingly involved with committee work in the Scout Movement; I'd organised coach trips to theatres to see Grand Opera and, among other hobby activities, made furniture at night-school. Now in 1963 I began to produce Scout Gang Shows and had also taken on the role as Business Manager to the newly-formed

Atherstone Amateur Operatic Society. Their previous production had been in 1929 with a performance of 'The Arcadians' in the old Picturedrome Cinema, but now with the new Memorial Hall as a venue the Society was re-born with Gilbert and Sullivan's "Trial by Jury" in 1963, followed by "The Mikado" in 1964. My less than adequate quiet tenor voice also enabled me to sing in with the 'Jury' in "Trial'", and be one of the 'gentlemen of Japan' in 'Titipu'.

In spite of all these interests – or because of them – I was doing well in my job, but to accept promotion would mean my leaving the town, and this appeared to be completely out of the question.

Returning from holiday at the end of July I was called to the District Office where I met my Divisional Manager who'd come specially to see me. He shook me by the hand and said,

"I want you to go to Burton-on-Trent as Assistant District Manager, alright?"

I accepted without a moment's hesitation. The next day was my country round and I called on that house in Sheepy. Before entering I composed myself and concentrated on looking and acting normally.

"You're going", she said before I had chance to speak..."you're leaving us, and you've 'shaken the shackles'!"

If Arthur Conan Doyle had been looking he would have been proud of her.

# CHAPTER ELEVEN

# OUT OF ATHERSTONE

Mr Abell sat looking at me across his desk in his office, fumbled for his cigarettes in his jacket pocket, lit one and inhaled deeply. His eyes twitched nervously as always when he was about to speak.

"Er – well John, you really can't go to Burton with your mini-van, so – um -"

I interrupted him and he seemed relieved.

"I've already given that some thought and I've made arrangements about getting a new Ford Anglia".

He continued, now appearing more relaxed. "Good – now this is what you have to do. First you resign from the Company, and then apply for the position of Assistant District Manager, so for a brief moment -" he smiled and gave a little chuckle, – "you're out of a job!"

He'd been my District Manager since I had started in December 1947, almost seventeen years ago, and was making a bit of a joke about a silly situation. In his job he always gave the appearance of being a worried man as the District rarely enjoyed any success or Divisional Honours. With Hinckley to the North of us and Foleshill to the South, both very successful and 'top' Districts, we in

Nuneaton were a bit like 'piggy-in-the-middle', and constantly reminded of our poor new business production as a District when visited by the Divisional Manager – much to the embarrassment of Mr Abell.

Always the gentleman, he was kind and considerate to the needs and welfare of his staff, which was believed to be by some District Managers at that time, almost the only necessary requirement of management to run a successful District.

However, there was a more positive attitude beginning to emerge among the field staff, who had previously resisted any change in the conventional way that life assurance was presented and sold. The potential of our business in an expanding market was seen by many to be full of opportunities, providing the staff were better trained in product knowledge and selling techniques.

This is how I saw the situation as I left my present position as District Agent, and with a new car and a new town, I was looking forward to the possibilities and challenges that lay ahead. I started my new job at the beginning of October 1964, bought a house in the village of Stretton on the outskirts of Burton-on-Trent, and we moved in just before Christmas.

Burton-on-Trent was a County Borough at that time with a population of about 50,000, of which a considerable number of the working population were employed by the breweries and allied industries. The Pearl did a lot of business with these people who, I found, were very loyal to their employers and proud of their traditions of making beer. One thing you could be certain of in the many public houses in the town, was always to get a 'fine glass of beer'. Much was drunk by some of the brewers while they were at work, especially in the warmth of the Propogation Plant where the yeast was 'grown'. It wasn't unusual for men to drink a few pints of beer before breakfast.

Along with other life assurance companies, the Pearl used to impose a small extra premium on policies issued under their

Ordinary Branch tables, for people engaged in the sale or manufacture of intoxication liquors. I was told that Burton policyholders had been exempt from these premium 'loadings' probably due to the fact that most of the people with whom we did business had been involved, or connected to, the brewing industry! After only a brief initiating period I was convinced that the quality of beer was such that it possibly lengthened life, not shortened it, and I applauded what had been the Company's policy!

Brewing was the oldest industry in Burton, dating back even prior to the monastic days of the 16th century. It remained as only a small-scale occupation until the 19th century when it expanded rapidly to 31 breweries employing 8,000 people. In 1964, the only breweries in the town were now the consortium of Ind Coope (Allied Breweries), and Bass and Marstons.

There were eight agents in the Burton-on-Trent office, four of them also calling in the villages around the town including historical Tutbury, and Repton on the other side of the River Trent. Two had their debits mainly in the town itself and the remaining two covered the South Derbyshire district of Swadlincote, which had a further population of approximately 40,000 people. Although only a short distant away from Burton, they were different people with different traditions. As coal mining was the main industry, I found that their way of life and attitudes were similar to those of the miners of Atherstone.

During my thirteen years at Burton, I had nine or ten changes of agency staff and two changes of District Manager. I was divorced, remarried and, before my son, David, was born in August 1976, I had been into hospital for three operations.

The first time was for a laminectomy, better known as a 'slipped disc' operation, but in spite of most of us in the ward having a certain amount of pain for a while, we had a lot of fun. In the next bed there was a lad with a badly-broken leg which was in plaster and on pulleys, restricting his movements. In another was a lorry driver from one of the breweries, with damaged ribs due to having had a beer barrel fall on him from his lorry. We heard the orthopaedic surgeon ask him if it was full!

"Full!" he exclaimed (well whispered really – he could hardly breathe)

"Full!, if it 'ad been full I'd have been squashed into the bloody tarmac!"

The fourth member of our 'squad' was an old boy who had had a cartilage operation and was getting better. He had been a stand-up comic when he was a young man and persisted in telling jokes and funny stories even though we were in no position to be able to laugh at them.

"Did you hear about the two women who met in the street and one said to the other . . . . ." Sometimes we'd put our fingers into our ears when he started because we knew how painful it was for us to laugh, but we could still hear him.

". . . . . where's your son these days, I haven't seen him for ages?"

"Oh didn't you know, he's in the army out East but he writes home sometimes . . . . . by the way, what's a brothel?"

"I think it's one of those places they have abroad", said the other, ". . . . . where you can get a bowl of broth".

"I thought that it might be", said the first, "because he wrote in his last letter that he'd been in to one the night before to have a basinful".

My hands would clench and my body stiffen in an effort not to laugh, the 'broken leg' would bite his lip and hold his suspended leg with both hands to try to prevent it from going up and down, and if 'the ribs' was out of bed, he would walk away his arms wrapped tightly round his body in an effort to control his breathing. After two or three jokes from George we were exhausted, through forcing ourselves not to laugh. As soon as we saw him look round to see if any nurses were about, and begin with, "Did you hear about....."we knew we were in trouble.

We vowed we would get our own back as soon as the opportunity presented itself and it did.....one afternoon when he was fast asleep. The vicar was doing his rounds and George was snoring.

"Anyone here for communion tomorrow?" he asked. If there was anyone in the hospital that could be labelled as blasphemous, it was George.

"Yes", we chorused, "George, only he's asleep at the moment".

"Tell him I'll be here early tomorrow morning".

We didn't tell him. When the vicar arrived next day and began to close the curtains around his bed, George's face was a picture. I believe he thought he was about to receive his last rites. We could hardly restrain ourselves as we listened to the quiet mutterings coming from behind the curtains.

My second visit to the hospital two-and-a-half years later, was for a vagotomy and pyloroplasty, (duodenal ulcer operation) followed by another couple of visits weeks later due to adhesions, which necessitated my third operation.

Fully recovered from these inconveniences, I began to do well in my job, and by the middle of 1977 I was second in the Division for Combined Life and the top ADM for premium content per policy. I was promoted to District Manager at Boston in the middle of July.

At that time I was living in Swadlincote, and until we were able to sell and move, I lodged at a guest house just outside Boston. It was a popular place with commercial travellers but mainly because of the cordiality of the previous owners: the present owner was a dour Scot and very moody, but his wife was of a much more pleasant disposition. He had the pay-phone removed from the hall and objected to his own being used by the guests. My wife rang early one evening before dinner to inform me that our son – he was then only a year old – was feeling much better after a bout of measles.

"Your wife's on the 'phone", he told me abruptly, then, after I had received the message, he followed me out of the room with "this isn't a public 'phone you know – I hope your wife's not going to make a habit of ringing you!"

The food was quite acceptable, but on one evening when only two of us were in for dinner he told us,

"My wife's cooked you two a treat tonight – potato croquettes".

When they arrived two of them lay on the plates, side by side, covered in hard breadcrumbs straight from the packet. We tried to eat them but it was like eating mashed potatoes dipped in sawdust! – they hadn't been fried. We were pleased that we were being 'treated' – we dreaded to think what we might have had if not.

Coffee was served in the lounge and there was always only the exact amount for one cup each in the pot. One evening after dinner when we entered the lounge, there was a couple from New Zealand sitting there looking quite forlorn. They told us that they were cycling round England, but owing to their late arrival they had been told that they were too late for a meal. Although they'd been there an hour or so they hadn't even been offered a drink so we insisted they had a cup of coffee each, which naturally left us short. Our 'friendly' proprietor came into the lounge – as he did most evenings to watch our television – and we asked him for some more coffee. He looked as though we'd asked him to buy the Crown Jewels, and then saw the cups in front the new visitors.

"They're not supposed to be having coffee!" he said, pointing his finger accusingly at them as he addressed us. We told him in no uncertain terms that we wanted some more and he grabbed the jug and returned with it with the exact quantity for two more cups. At times he could be quite pleasant but his main fault was to burn the breakfast toast. "I've had enough of this", said a regular visitor one morning and proceeded to scrape the burnt black surface all over the tablecloth. Next day the toast showed a great improvement. Fortunately I was coming to the end of my stay but some of the commercial travellers who had stayed there for many years vowed that they wouldn't return. However, we always saw the funny side of the situations and had many a good laugh.

I knew little or nothing about the county of Lincolnshire except that it was mainly agricultural around the town of Boston. I was also aware that this part of England, and 'The Wash' in particular, was rich in wild bird life, and I was looking forward to working and living in a completely different area and environment. We had passed through the town some years previously on our way to Skegness in a friend's car, and I remembered the little-owls sitting on telegraph wires on our way to the seaside resort. Now I was going to live and work there and as well as meeting Building Society Managers and local business men, which I felt was important in my new job as District Manager, I thought that I ought to find out something about the history of the town.

The Lincolnshire town of Boston as an East Coast Port at the beginning of the 13th century was second only to London with both coastal and European trade. By 1300 it was considered to be England's leading port, contributing a third more in customs duties than London. The gradual importance as a North Sea port declined for a number of reasons, not least due to the silting up of the river in the 15th century.

In 1766 the Grand Sluice on the River Witham was opened and the river deepened. When the Dock was built in 1882, a 'new Cut' was made for the Witham, which straightened and deepened the shipping channel. Since when it has always done a large trade in timber with the continent.

Along the banks of the Witham stands a Monument recalling the first attempt made by the Pilgrim Fathers to leave England in search of religious freedom in 1607. Erected by Boston Borough Council in 1957, it stands near to the place that the Pilgrims arranged to board a ship in which they hoped to reach the Low Countries. Unfortunately for them, the captain of the ship betrayed their presence to the authorities at Boston just when they were on the point of sailing. They were removed from the vessel by officers of the port and imprisoned in the town, under an act of parliament in force at that time which made unauthorized emigration illegal.

The cells where the leaders of the Pilgrims were held for a while are still there in the Guildhall, which is now a museum. Close to, is the lovely little Blackfriars Theatre, ingeniously constructed in the 1960's in a near-ruined building which had been the refectory of a Dominican Friary.

The outstanding building in Boston is also the largest Parish Church in England and is dedicated to St.Botolph. The lantern-tower is affectionately known as Boston Stump, though no one knows how it came to be so called. It is over 270 feet high and took seventy years to construct in the 15th century.

In the January following my arrival, the town suffered very severe flooding. A flood mark on a buttress to the right of the west door of the tower shows that the church was flooded throughout to a depth of 18 inches. It was the highest recorded water level and the flood washed away the river bank and caused a lot of water damage to houses where we called. I made special arrangements with our claims department to make immediate payments in order to relieve the hardship suffered by our policyholders.

The District Office was situated above a supermarket near to the centre of the town and close to where an auction-market was held on Wednesdays. Here one could buy almost anything from a rusty lawnmower to a box of lettuce, and on more than one occasion, I even saw an old car or two being sold by the auctioneers.

We covered an area of over 600 square miles with agents as far from the office as Skegness and Mablethorpe. I had an excellent staff and enjoyed every minute of the six years I was manager of the District until I was transferred (in 1983) to the much larger District of Grimsby, from where I retired seven years later.

While at Boston I received word that my father was seriously ill. He was in a coma when I arrived at his bedside in the front room at home – the same room from where I used to watch it rain and where we listened to that memorable broadcast by Neville

Chamberlain forty-four years earlier.

Seeing him lying there with his eyes closed reminded me of when I had seen him in hospital immediately following his accident involving a motor-cyclist when he was aged seventy. When the rider had been brought to the court, Dad had seen the funny side of the proceedings as usual, and had given a hilarious account of the events.

"A witness was called to give evidence on what he saw, but when he tried to explain how the motor-cyclist overtook a car, he got his off-side and his near-side confused and then into a further mess with his left and his right. In an effort to try and sort it out, the chairman of the magistrates asked him,

'Mr B....., if you were cycling down Long Street, which side of the road would you be on, the right or the left?'

"Mr B..... looked thoughtful, and then as the light dawned on what was required of him, and in an effort to be accurate with his answer said,

'But I don't ride a bike sir!'"

After the motor-cycle had crashed into Dad as he had been walking along the pavement, he suffered a lot of pain because of the bruising and a broken ankle he had received, but apart from the first few days he had remained cheerful. To make the best of it and always look on the bright side had been his philosophy throughout his life, not only during his numerous and painful operations for his spina-bifida problems but also following his other misfortunes.

There was the time when he had fallen down three steps outside the house very early one morning on his way to catch the train to work. He had walked with difficulty the half mile to the station, then another quarter of a mile from Coundon Station to the Alvis Works only to be brought home immediately as unable to work, due to a very badly swollen knee. During the black-out, he again had leg injuries when he got off the train at Atherstone which hadn't pulled up fully to the platform, and yet another accident in his Stores department, in an 'arguement' with a wheelbarrow!

He had an operation to remove polypi following a spate of severe nose bleeds, and another spell in Keresley Hospital with conjunctivitis, yet his humour and cheerful attitude always won through whatever the situation.

His working days at Coventry during the war were long, and during the days of the blitz along with his fellow workers, dangerous also. They were journeying home one evening in the pitch dark when an air-raid started. The train stopped as it was instructed to do, but unfortunately right alongside the gas-works. Naturally, the passengers thought they now presented an even bigger target for the bombs to hit.

"If 'Jerry' had hit the stationary train," Dad told us, "we'd have all been blown up, but if he'd have hit the gas works, we'd have all been blown up higher!"

Never a big man, his body now looked very small and frail as I tried to make him more comfortable and detected a faint squeeze of the hand as if in recognition of what I was doing. He was a man of peace. I never saw him angry, lose his temper or heard him swear.

He died that night on 15th December 1979 in Nuneaton hospital aged ninety-two.

I moved to Grimsby in April 1983 and, wishing to find out a little more about the town I had come to live and work in, I visited the auction sale at the fish market early one morning on the docks. It was fascinating to see the speed at which the fish was sold to the men in the white coats although I hardly saw a bid being made! I watched a vessel being unloaded and the fish sorted by the 'lumpers', and talked to the 'filleters' and 'splitters' preparing the fish for sale. Although Grimsby has declined from being world famous as a centre of the fishing industry, it is now recognised as the leading centre for the processing and quick freezing of fish, fruit, vegetables, poultry and other foodstuffs.

At first I wondered whether I had done the right thing in accepting the move to a much larger District, but I soon found the job much more interesting and a greater challenge to me. All the staff had a good working knowledge, enthusiastic and dedicated to their work, and the agents successful. Although there were inevitably a few set-backs in the seven years I was there, these were quickly overcome and the District made good progress towards the Company's objectives. But the Pearl was changing, and new management with a different approach was reorganising the way that the Company was run and how Districts performed. In addition, new technology was being introduced, accounting procedures changed and computers installed into the offices. I decided to retire following my sixty-second birthday having completed forty-two years with the Company.

I now planned to do all the things I had been unable to devote much time to when working. I had already formed an RSPB (Royal Society for the Protection of Birds) Members' Group in preparation for retirement, and looked forward to taking a greater interest in wild birds. This interest probably began when I took part in the RSPB 'Bird and Tree Competition' at school. It had been stimulated by programmes on the radio such as 'Nature Parliament', under the chairmanship of 'Uncle Mac' (Donald McCulloch) and with panellists, Bruce Campbell, James Fisher and Peter Scott as the ornithological experts and the authority on butterflies, L. B. Newman. They had dealt with questions sent in, mainly by children and their answers and observations had been meticulously precise. On one occasion, Bruce Campbell had described how he had been watching a black-headed gull feeding, and noted that in a five minute period, the bird made over fifty stabs with its bill of which thirty-seven were followed by a swallow! Other impetus was probably provided by a complementary programme, 'Out with Romany' in which all kinds of wild life were observed. Both were, of course, before the advent of television when we would be able to watch programmes on nature for ourselves.

Members' Groups were formed with the purpose to promote the aims and help with the work of the Royal Society for the Protection of Birds in the local community. The idea of the formation of a group in Grimsby was raised at the annual RSPB Film Show by the East Midlands Regional Officer, Martin Davis, and with the encouragement of his assistant, Richard Campey, I formed a small committee in the summer of 1986. We held our inaugural meeting in September of that year at the Winter Gardens in Cleethorpes and, much to our delight and surprise, 250 people turned up.

During the next six years we produced regular Newsletters for all 1500 RSPB members in our area, keeping them informed of our activities. We organised a monthly programme of illustrated talks from every September to May, arranged outside events at Garden Centres, Parks and Reserves Sites, raised money, enrolled new members and tried to make more people aware of the need to protect wild birds and their habitat. In addition, we gave talks to Church Groups, Youth Organisations, Schools, W. I's and other similar groups, and gave a couple of short interviews on local radio. We supported our local Reserve at Tetney marshes – some 3100 acres of intertidal mud and sandflats, saltmarsh and sand-dunes – and organised the annual Open Day. The Summer Warden's main job is to protect the Little Terns which nest there: because they nest low on the sands, their nests have to be lifted on to boxes and then replaced during the spring tides. Foxes are deterred from egg-snatching by an electric fence. Starting in mid-May, over 90 pairs of terns nested in 1987, and many chicks had hatched by July. Despite the vagaries of the weather that year, about 80 finally fledged – which was a record. The site has recently been purchased by the Society and the work continues for the Little Terns.

The whole of the coast near to Grimsby and Cleethorpes is a wonderful area for bird watching and the Humber Estuary is the fourth most important estuary in Britain for wintering waders and wildfowl. Birds such as knot, dunlin and brent geese come in their thousands to the Estuary after having bred in the remote tundra areas north of the Artic Circle. I once counted over 400 curlew on the mud-flats not far from the Grimsby Dock-Tower.

Further up the Humber, at the point where the rivers Ouse and Trent meet, lies Blacktoft Sands RSPB Reserve. It was here in 1837, at the last recognised avocets' breeding site in Great Britain, that the last two pairs had been shot and their eggs stolen. It was not until 1947 – following the deliberate flooding of the land in an area of Suffolk during the war as a barrier against potential invasion – that avocets returned to this country to breed again. The Society was keen to protect the marsh, and so Minsmere reserve was born. The avocet symbol was first used as the RSPB's Logo in 1955, but not until the 1960s was it made into a proper design with the RSPB initials. At Blacktoft, in the late 1980s, the avocet was seen again visiting the reserve and in 1992 a pair nested. In the evening of the day that Andrew Grieve celebrated his 21st year as warden of the site, and also his 25 years with the RSPB, he discovered an egg in the avocet's nest – the first avocet's egg at Blacktoft for 155 years! They have bred ever since.

In the May of that year, the Members' Group was the strongest it had been and the committee was working with commitment and enthusiasm, so I felt that it was time to retire as Leader and Chairman and hand over to someone else. Over the years we sent (to the Society) many thousands of pounds which we had raised from Grand Draws, raffles, sale of goods, bird seed and nuts. By obtaining sponsorship from local firms, we were also able to make a good profit from our monthly meetings. The Group still flourishes and continues to have great success with their fund raising.

I would now have more time to pursue my other hobbies and interests as well, including golf, which I had taken up before leaving Boston. I had a lot to look forward to and if I was going to take after my parents for longevity (Mother born in 1900 and still alive in

1994) I had a lot of planning to do, not least to write a story about the times that I had lived through.

# CHAPTER THIRTEEN

# CONCLUSION

When I had almost finished this story of my life, I had an urge to go back and visit the town where I had spent the first thirty-six years.

I arrived in Atherstone on Shrove Tuesday (1994) before the 'Ball Game' started. The 'Blue Bell' from where the ball had been 'thrown out' for all the years I could remember – had gone. The Regal Cinema, where we had queued waiting for seats on Sunday evenings in the 1940s, was no longer there either. All the Hat Factories, except one, where a large proportion of the people of the town had worked, had been pulled down – and everyone I met had aged thirty years!

I searched in vain for the familiar faces of shop-keepers. A few of the names on the shop fronts remained but the owners had changed. Parts of the canal had been drained and sections had disappeared altogether. The Outwoods had overgrown. I wondered whether young boys still rode their imaginary horses up and down the hills, or if they now sat with their eyes 'glued' to that magic box in the corner of their living rooms instead?

Shrove Tuesday was a good day for meeting lots of people, and I was greeted warmly by old friends and school chums – and yet I felt a stranger in my own home town. I also met again a couple of the lads (now in their 40's) who had been young scouts in our first Gang Show. In spite of my ruthless treatment of them during rehearsals, they remembered the times with affection.

"I still remember all the words", said one.

"They were great days", said the other.

When I arrived back in the town, I had thought that I would still feel that I belonged, as my roots were there, but I had been away too long. I had moved out of Atherstone and I couldn't go back. I didn't want to. My life had been spent away from the town for too many years, and only memories remained.